Health and Medicine in the Islamic Tradition

Health/Medicine and the Faith Traditions

Edited by Martin E. Marty and Kenneth L. Vaux

Health/Medicine and the Faith Traditions
explores the ways in which major religions
relate to the questions of human well-being.
It issues from Project Ten, an interfaith program
of The Park Ridge Center, An Institute for the Study of
Health, Faith, and Ethics.

James P. Wind, Director of Research and Publications

The Park Ridge Center
is part of the Lutheran General Health Care System,
Park Ridge, Illinois.

Health and Medicine in the Islamic Tradition

CHANGE AND IDENTITY

Fazlur Rahman

Crossroad • New York

1987
The Crossoad Publishing Company
370 Lexington Ave, New York, N.Y. 10017

Printed in the United States of America

Library of Congress Cataloging in Publication Data

Rahman, Fazlur, 1919–
Health and medicine in the Islamic tradition.

(Health/medicine and the faith traditions)
Includes Index.
1. Medicine—Religious aspects—Islam. 2. Health—Religious aspects—Islam. I. Title. II. Series.
[DNLM: 1. Ethics, Medical. 2. Islam. 3. Religion and Medicine. W 50 R147h]
BP166.72.R35 1987 297'.1975 87–6732
ISBN 0–8245–0797–5

To the memory of my parents

"Lord! have your mercy on them even as they tenderly brought me up when I was little."
Qur'an 17, 24

Contents

Foreword

I first read the manuscript for this book in leisure hours during a conference at which Fazlur Rahman spoke. Participants in the conference converged on one of those buzzwords that tend to be favored at such gatherings, the word *perspective*. Thus philosopher Peter Winch speaks of perspective: "There is no way of getting outside the concepts in terms of which we think of the world. . . . The world *is* for us what is presented through those concepts."

Such an issue of perspective came to mind as we heard Professor Rahman speak. He reflected the Muslim world from which he came and to which he devotes a scholarly career. At the same time he is very much at home in a modern pluralist university and society, where he knows he must—as he does in this book—explain his concepts to people who come with perspectives that do not mirror Islamic life. He had to beckon us into his world. Only then did many elements that might otherwise seem implausible begin to take on the appearance of coherence.

Muslim readers of this book, of which we hope there will be many, will bring their perspectives to it. They will judge the work in the light of their experiences, which include familiarity with the Qur'an and the long traditions of the prophetic faith of Islam. No doubt they will debate the accuracy of Professor Rahman's history, the fairness of his judgments, the appropriateness of his canons of relevance. If past reception of his work is any guide, we can be confident that this book will be favorably reviewed and will find wide acceptance. Non-Muslim readers can know that they are in the hands of a world-renowned expert on Islam.

Health and Medicine in the Islamic Tradition is the first book in this series to deal with a religious movement whose members are for the most part outside the Euro-American sphere. Islam is out there, or over there. Islamdom abuts Christendom more than it overlaps it. Where there was overlapping of the sort that occurred at both ends of the Mediterranean, there was chiefly conflict and misunderstanding. There is an Islamic world, and it is not here.

So a public is likely to think. It is true that the Muslim faith has generated a world. In the middle of the twentieth century, every seventh human was Muslim. A third of a century later, every fifth human followed Islam or bore its name. This change results from population growth as well as from strenuous conversion efforts. Much of the expansion of Islam has occurred not at its apathetic edges but around its aggressive center. "Islamic fundamentalism" has become a household word.

To concentrate only on the Islam that makes front-page news in a world of tension and terror, however, is to distort the role this faith plays in the lives of millions. The majority of Muslims do not follow the faith in order to prepare themselves for a *jihād.* They do not want to start wars against pagans and infidels. Most of them are Muslim because they were born to the faith or were converted by the efforts of other believers. They hold to it because they know no other way, are at home with no other concepts, have no other perspective; many who have sampled alternatives return to it.

Islam, like other religions, exerts its hold because it addresses and in many ways satisfies longings and desires of people—for experience, authority, and identity, for meaning in a world that they cannot grasp in random fashion. This book shows how extensive is the reach of this faith into the dimensions of private and public life embraced by the title of this series: "Health and Medicine."

It may surprise the reader that Professor Rahman speaks of his book as the first of its sort. Libraries are full of literature that comments on this or that aspect of the subject, yet there have been no collations of the main themes of the tradition. It may also surprise the reader to learn how profound, elaborate, and intricate are the elements of Islam that do have a bearing on health and medicine. The Qur'an, the revelation which is at the basis of this faith, does not seem to have many directly relevant passages. Yet Muslims through the centuries have searched these passages, the commentaries that grew in the early centuries, the treatises from the various Muslim sects, the stories attributed to the career of the prophet Muhammad, and other elements of the tradition in order to relate their search for well-being to the all-important demand that they follow the will of God. One can stand at a great distance and be awed by how much there is to know in and about the Islamic world. To be drawn to its perspective will be, for most outsiders, to confront a world that threatens, enthralls, puzzles, and inspires. I found this book to be intrinsically of interest, even if it is construed as having to do with faraway places and distant times. It would not have to be practical at all in order to command attention.

Even in America, however, writing such as this no longer sounds so arcane or remote. Understanding health and medicine in the Islamic tradition has become a matter of practical concern. The Muslim is no longer by any means contained in certain geographic areas. He or she has moved next door.

It is hard to estimate how many Muslims are now in North America. The guesses range from 2 to 5 million. While this figure includes some members of unorthodox groups like the Black Muslims or the "Nation of Islam," many other blacks are orthodox followers of the Qur'an. Meanwhile, there have been through the decades slow and subtle migrations of people from the Muslim world, not least notably in recent times of unrest, people of varied fortunes. Many came as students and remained as professionals. Others represented foreign commercial firms and established long-term residency in the United States and Canada, or they changed their employment and took out citizenship papers.

The students who now populate American colleges and universities are often more self-conscious about their Islamic practice than were many who preceded them. These are days in which people put a premium on their identity. They affirm their roots and sympathize with many kinds of national and ethnic movements abroad. Campuses allow for refinement of philosophical and religious outlooks and have often become organizing centers for Muslim self-consciousness. This trend is likely to continue in America as Muslims bring and acquire wealth and express power. One is as likely to find Muslim worship in suburbs as in cities, in upper-class white enclaves as in black communities. If present trends continue, before many decades pass Muslims will outnumber Jews and become the second largest faith group in America. The Muslim next door has to be understood. His or her attitudes toward health and medicine will help inform such understanding.

Those who now deliver health care will be serving more Muslim patients, whose concepts of their body, diet, and practices will appear on diagnostic charts. Conversely, many Islamic professionals are in the medical world. Although they may have completed their training in the United States and may comprehend the best in modern scientific care and technological treatment, they also will represent the perspectives of Muslim faith and culture. Professor Rahman's work is crucial at this stage in helping North Americans understand the concepts of illness, well-being, suffering, and destiny that live in the Muslim mind and world.

I have resisted commenting on the content of the chapters that follow. It is necessary to follow the author as he creates, with words, a world. Then one can follow its labyrinthine corridors, survey its libraries and clinics, and make sense of what will at first seem obscure. What I know about Muslim concepts of health and medicine I have learned chiefly from earlier work of Fazlur Rahman as well as from the work in hand, to which the reader now has access. It is time to step aside in respect to admire and profit from the perspective of this scholar and friend—and then, one hopes, to have a basis for informed dissent or consent. Both where Muslim meanings intersect with those of other faiths and cultures and where they go their own way entirely, they can serve to jostle new thought among people who come from many perspectives. If so, the modest author will have achieved far more than his understated, matter-of-fact work suggests he set out to do. He will have contributed to well-being, also among those who may never come to share the perspective.

Martin E. Marty

Prefatory Note

The following pages represent an attempt to portray the relationship of Islam as a system of faith and as a tradition to human health and health care: What value does Islam attach to human well-being—spiritual, mental, and physical—and what inspiration has it given Muslims to realize that value? The work, therefore, is *not* a history of medicine in Islam, although Chapter 4 does provide information about Islamic health institutions in order to furnish an adequate measure for judging Islam's actual performance.

Islamic medicine has not before been systematically approached from this perspective. General works on Islamic medicine—although there are good ones—can hardly claim to touch meaningfully upon the subject: its vastness demands far greater effort to do justice to it. This monograph, then, must be regarded only as a modest beginning.

My thanks are due to Professor C. M. Naim of the Department of South Asian Languages and Civilizations of the University of Chicago and to the staff of the Regenstein Library at the University of Chicago (Middle Eastern and South Asian sections), particularly Fayez Sayegh, for helping to locate certain materials and references. The translations from the original sources (Arabic, Persian, Turkish, and Urdu) are all my own.

A Historical Introduction to Islam

The name of the last of the great Semitic religions, Islam, literally means "to submit to God's will or law." It was promulgated by Muhammad, son of 'Abd Allah, born in 570 C.E. in Mecca, in the clan of Banū Hāshim belonging to the powerful tribe of Quraish. The Quraish had settled in this town about 150 years before the Prophet Muhammad's birth and had gained prosperity through a flourishing trade between Byzantium and the Indian Ocean. Also, Mecca housed the Ka'ba, the object of annual pilgrimage for Arabs. Before his call to prophethood, Muhammad was a trader, and at the age of twenty-five, he married a rich widow named Khadīja, whose business he managed. After marriage, he was in the habit of retiring to a cave called Ḥirā' to contemplate the problems of life and death but particularly the problems that existed in Meccan society, namely, polytheism and a grave socioeconomic imbalance between the rich and the very poor. At about the age of forty, Muhammad received the call in one of his moods of contemplation in the cave and launched a struggle to establish monotheism and to rectify the socioeconomic disequilibrium—the two basic pillars of his mission. Mecca's powerful aristocracy resisted him and persecuted him and his band of followers, who were mainly drawn from the poor and disenfranchised classes. After more than a decade of preaching in Mecca, he emigrated to the town of Medina (in pre-Islamic times called Yathrib), where the two Arab tribes, long locked in feuding, invited him to be their ruler. The Prophet, as the supreme ruler of Medina, instituted a series of reforms and laid the foundations of the nascent Islamic state. Thus, besides the religious doctrines and duties promulgated by him as God's prophet, the sphere of the state and the public sector of life also became part of the religion of Islam from the very beginning. Islam, therefore, never envisaged, until very recently (and then only in Turkey), the division between the public life on the one hand and a private religion on the other; rather, the entire fabric of Islamic life, both private and public, is governed by the laws of Islam.

Muhammad died in June 632 C.E. after practically the whole of Arabia had embraced the religion of Islam. He was succeeded by rulers after him who were titled caliphs (the word *caliph* means "successor"). The caliphs, who were executive heads of the religious community of Islam but without any religious prerogatives to enunciate laws or define dogma, expanded the domain of Islam within a century after the Prophet's death from the shores of the Atlantic in North Africa deep into Central Asia up to India. A legal system was required for the administration of this vast empire, and the jurists of Islam gradually formulated a comprehensive law during the first three centuries of Islam; thus law was the first Islamic discipline to come into being. Eventually, four schools of Sunni law and one school of Shi'a law (the latter is now operative in Iran) emerged. The Sunni-Shi'a division began early in Islam because some Muslims felt that the rightful successor to the Prophet Muhammad was not Abū Bakr, whom the majority had acclaimed as their ruler, but 'Alī, cousin and son-in-law of the Prophet. 'Alī was, however, elected as the fourth caliph by the community. The Shi'a began as a political schism and became, over the course of time, a religious sect with their own theology and legal system. At the present, of the approximately one billion Muslims in the world, around 60–70 million are Shi'a, largely in Iran and Iraq, but also scattered in India, Syria, Lebanon, and eastern Turkey.

The definitive sources of Islamic doctrine and practice are two: the Qur'an and the Sunna. The Qur'an consists of the messages which the Prophet Muhammad received from Allah from 610, the year of his call, until he died in 632. These passages were collected and recorded during his own lifetime. But the Qur'an was also memorized by many Muslims, sometimes in its entirety. It was daily recited in prayers. The text that we now possess was collected and arranged during the caliphate of the third caliph, 'Uthmān (d. 656), and has remained intact throughout Islamic history. It comprises 114 suras, or chapters, of unequal length. The longest suras, which actually originated later, stand at the beginning of the vulgate edition, while the short suras, which were actually the first to be revealed, appear at the end. The Qur'an has been the source from which Muslims have derived not only their law and theology but also principles and institutions of their public life. It has been translated into all the major languages of the world and has appeared in a large number of English translations in recent years.

The second definitive source of Islam, after the Qur'an, is the Sunna of the Prophet. The term *sunna* means the example or model for others to follow. The Sunna, therefore, purportedly gives us the precepts and actions of the Prophet Muhammad outside the Qur'an. The reports through which these precepts and deeds are conveyed are called Ḥadīths. During the ninth century C.E., six collections of Ḥadīths were made by eminent Muslim scholars; these have been canonized as "genuine" Ḥadīths. The Shi'a have their own collections of Ḥadīths, dating from about a half-century after the Sunni Ḥadīth compilations. Some Ḥadīths are common to both the Sunni and the Shi'a, but whereas the Sunni Ḥadīths normally go back to the Prophet Muhammad, almost 90 percent of the Shi'a Ḥadīths go back to the Shi'a imams. The orthodox Shi'a (as opposed to extremist Shi'a subsects) believe in a series of twelve imams or supreme religiopolitical leaders held by them to be infallible and impeccable. The first imam is 'Alī, son-in-law of the Prophet, followed by his two sons, Ḥasan and Ḥusain. Ḥusain revolted against the Umayyad state based in Damascus and died fighting against government troops in the year 671. The death of Ḥusain was a turning point in the Shi'a religious ethos and introduced into Shi'ism the element of passion and the ideal of martyrdom. The nine imams followed after Ḥusain from his progeny, and the last is said to have disappeared in 873; his return is still awaited by the Shi'a. Because the orthodox Shi'a believe in twelve imams, they are called "Twelvers."

Besides the Twelver Shi'a, Shi'ism gave rise to several other subsects, the most important of which are the Ismā'īlīs. These are so called because they recognize as imam Ismā'īl, a son of the sixth imam, Ja'far al-Ṣādiq. Ismā'īl was not recognized by the Twelver Shi'a, however, because he had committed the sin of drinking alcohol; the Twelvers recognized instead his younger brother. The Ismā'īlīs have led the most successful revolutionary movement in Islam; they aimed at abrogating all the religious laws and, at the advent of the Mahdī (the last imam who would return toward the end of time), would institute a new religious era with a universal religion. The Ismā'īlī movement, because of its revolutionary character, had a subterranean life, propagating its esoteric views only to those whom it considered trustworthy. During the tenth century C.E., Ismā'īlīs built up a large empire stretching from North Africa and including Egypt and several other parts of the Muslim world like Yemen. However, after the establishment of their empire, they seemed to forget their revolutionary zeal and settled down as a status quo government. At the present time, the Ismā'īlī community is divided into two: the Bohras, who have their imam in Bombay and are centered in and around Bombay for the most part, and the larger community, the followers of the Aga Khan, who settled mainly in Kenya but immigrated to other parts of the world after Kenya's independence from British rule and are now largely in Toronto, Canada.

The first schism in Islam started very early, about two and a half decades after the Prophet's death, when the third caliph 'Uthmān was assassinated in his home by rebels who accused him of nepotism and grave maladministration. Debate ensued as to whether 'Uthmān's murder was justifiable. While some members of the community were noncommittal, a large number believed that the murder was unjustified. But others thought that the killing could be justified because 'Uthmān had committed grave errors. These people, later called the Khārijites, held that any Muslim who commits a grave sin or error but does not repent—that is, does not mend his actual behavior—becomes an infidel no matter how many times he professes the faith of Islam ("There is no god but Allah and Muhammad is his messenger"), prays, and fasts. The Khārijites took an extraordinarily fanatical stand and declared war on the Muslim community because, in their eyes, the entire Muslim community, in refusing to accept that 'Uthmān and others like him had become infidels, had itself become infidel. This stand was soon countered by the Murji'ites, who held that any sane person who, without trying to deceive others by lying, professes the Islamic faith is a Muslim and may not be excommunicated. As for whether his or her deeds are good or evil, the final judgment will be passed by God on the Day of Judgment, and it is not up to a human to judge another human in an ultimate sense. The Murji'ite stand was actually a bid for the solidarity of the community which was threatened by the Khārijite rebellionism. Both the Sunnis and the Shi'a accepted a moderate form of Murji'ism.

After these early sectarian opinions, the first systematic school of Islamic theology was that of the Mu'tazilites, which arose in the first half of the eighth century. The Mu'tazilites held that a Muslim who is guilty of a heinous crime (like theft, murder, or adultery) ceases to be a Muslim but does not become an infidel either: he occupies "a position between these two positions." The Mu'tazilites called themselves "People of God's Unity and Justice." By God's unity they meant that God is only an essence without attributes; if one conceives of God as having eternal attributes besides his essence, one is guilty of polytheism. The Mu'tazilites were on the frontiers of Islam, waging controversies with followers of other religions like Christianity, Buddhism, and Judaism. It appears that while controverting other religions, the Mu'tazilites also imbibed certain influences from them. Their doctrine of the Divine Essence and Attributes appears to have been palpably influenced by Christian discussions on the nature of the trinity and how three persons make up one God. As for their doctrine of the justice of God, they taught that God, because he is just, has given fully free and efficacious will to humans who alone, therefore, are responsible for their actions, *wherein God plays no role.* They further believed that just as God cannot punish good-doers in the hereafter, he cannot forgive evil-doers because otherwise the distinction between good and evil would evaporate. Because the Qur'an is full of verses emphasizing the limitless mercy and forgiveness of God, denied by the Mu'tazilites, the community in general came to disapprove strongly of their creed. After having been established state creed for several decades in the ninth century, it was brought down from power during the time of the caliph al-Mutawakkil (d. 861).

Against the extreme Mu'tazilite rationalism a reaction arose, spearheaded by the theologian al-Ash'arī (d. 942), who had first been a partisan of the Mu'tazilite school but later came under the influence of the rising Sunni religious world view largely based upon the Ḥadīth. Ash'arism, however, in its opposition to Mu'tazilitism, went to the other extreme. Whereas the Mu'tazilites had emphasized the justice of God and his unity, the Ash'arites emphasized the absolute will and power of God. Because God is omnipotent, they held, nothing else can be potent, neither nature nor humankind. Hence they denied causation and believed that what we human beings perceive as causation, the production of one thing by another, is actually a habitual behavior of God. For God habitually behaves this way, although if he chose, he could behave in different or even opposite ways. This theory, when transferred from the sphere of nature to the sphere of religion, produced embarrassing views. The Ash'arites, for example, held that there is no objective moral law, but that good and evil are determined by God (unlike the Mu'tazilites, who had held the opposite view). For the Ash'arites, it just happens that God has declared lying and murder to be evil, but if he had chosen, he could have declared them to be good. Good and evil, therefore, cannot be known from nature but must be discovered and learned from revelation (for this purpose, revelation of course does not mean just the revelation of Muhammad in the Qur'an, but the entire process of divine revelation beginning with Adam, the first man). The Ash'arite views remained the dominant theological tradition throughout Islamic history until well into the twentieth century and had effects upon scientific and particularly medical theory and practice, as will be discussed below.

Even before the activity of the lawyers and the theologians reached its fruition in the late third and early fourth centuries of Islam, a quite different phenomenon had already begun to take shape in the second century. Sufism (Islamic mysticism) represents the spiritual manifestation of Islam par excellence. Sufism seems to have arisen among certain spiritually sensitive individuals and circles, partly as a reaction to the development of general worldliness in the Muslim community with the new power and prosperity that the Empire had brought in, but even more so, perhaps, as a reaction against the formulation of Islam in legal and theological terms. For the Sufis argued that Islam essentially deals with the inner life of man, with the "tendence of the soul." Neither lawyers nor theologians cared for this side of religion, which for the Sufi was its essence. In its first phase, Sufism was mainly a manifestation of an ascetic piety, insisting on the purity of the heart and the moral cleanliness of the motivation of actions. It taught *zuhd*, detaching one's heart from the temptations of this life's luxuries and devoting oneself entirely to God. From these ascetic beginnings, Sufism developed its practice of *dhikr*, or "remembrance of God," which is so frequently emphasized in the Qur'an. By the practice of the constant remembrance of God, the Sufi began to cultivate an ecstatic ideal of love of God, in which union was sought with the Divine Being. During their ecstatic moods, known as the state of *sukr*, or intoxication, several Sufis made statements about the identification of their selves with God, which appeared extremely blasphemous to the orthodox. In 922, one of the most illustrious representatives of Sufism, al-Ḥallāj, was crucified in Baghdad after his hands and feet had been severed, and he was subsequently decapitated. Later Islamic generations have never forgotten this execution, and al-Ḥallāj has been recognized as the greatest martyr for divine love. The Sufis, in turn, gradually formulated ways of describing their ecstatic experiences that, although they did not compromise the Sufi experience and its content, nevertheless afforded justification for them to the orthodox, among them being the principle stated by many great Sufis that statements made by a Sufi in the state of "intoxication" cannot be taken at face value and that when the Sufi returns from that state "to this world," his interpretation of that experience is to be accepted as valid.

Sufism eventually arrived at the theosophical doctrine that there is only one being or principle of existence, of which the absolute representative is the transcendent God, while all other beings are modes and forms of that one principle of existence. This doctrine of the Unity of Being, or monism, exerted such an irresistible attraction that it became the virtual creed of later generations. The greatest formulator and representative of this theosophical Sufism was the Spanish Ibn 'Arabī, who died in Aleppo in 1240. Ibn 'Arabī has left us numerous works, but his magnum opus is the *Meccan Disclosures*, a massive collection of his mystical experiences and analyses, which he claimed to have received during his stay in Mecca. This theosophical Sufism, while avoiding crass pantheism, nevertheless is straightforwardly monistic. Its main ideas became common stock for Persian, Turkish, and Urdu poetry in the following centuries, with an immense influence on Arabic poetry as well. This poetry, particularly the Persian, with its rich quasi-pantheistic allusions and symbols and masterful artistry, remains among the most beautiful poetic performances of the human race; it often disregarded the sensibilities of the orthodox religion and indeed ridiculed orthodox ritualism and formalism. Sufis cultivated a broad humanism and latitudinarianism; they helped all human beings irrespective of their creeds. Their attitudes also made for moral and spiritual relativism, justifying all the systems of religious beliefs and human creeds held throughout the historic past. Although this stance was anathema to the orthodox, nevertheless when looked at closely, it is not so far from the teaching of the Qur'an itself, which recurrently upholds the view that God has not left any people or nation on the earth without guidance and that divine guidance is not a special or exclusive prerogative of Jews, Christians, and Muslims. The Qur'an does, however, assert that there has been evolution in religion and that the Qur'an is the highest embodiment of divine guidance and revelation, while all other religions, though containing fundamental truths, have been sometimes corrupted and overlaid with false interpretations.

From the twelfth century onward, Sufism developed into a mass phenomenon in the form of Sufi Orders or Brotherhoods organized throughout the Muslim world. Sufi hospices (*zāwiyas*, *tekkes*, or *khāngahs*) mushroomed. In such a hospice a Sufi shaikh initiated and guided his elect disciples into the spiritual path; he also gave counsel to the common people not only on spiritual and religious questions but on worldly difficulties and problems as well. Orthodox religious scholars—the same theologians and lawyers who had scoffed at and opposed Sufism in the early stages of its development—began enrolling in Sufi orders from about the thirteenth and fourteenth centuries. The acceptability of Sufism was facilitated by certain outstanding individuals who had adopted the Sufi path but were at the same time firmly grounded in Islamic theology and law. The most illustrious in this connection is Abū Ḥāmid al-Ghazālī (d. 1111), who in his early career was a famed professor of Islamic law and theology at the Niẓāmīya College in Baghdad but resigned his post in the midst of glory and success, overcome by a spiritual crisis. For years he wandered in Syria and Egypt, living alone in cells in mosques and hospices until he wrote his great work, *The Revivification of Religious Sciences*.

Sufism made Muslims generally passive, but the representatives of Islamic law and theology in the later medieval centuries had done hardly better in supplying Muslims with dynamism. Both law and theology after their systematization during the tenth and eleventh centuries became static. Originality was sternly discouraged, presumably because both law and theology in their early development had passed through stormy differences of opinion on almost all points and the orthodoxy did not want the basic questions, once they had become uniform and standardized, to be reopened for discussion. From the thirteenth century on, we confront a period of commentaries and supercommentaries which signaled the loss of originality on basic issues. Certainly, much ingenuity and even originality lies buried in these commentaries, but the main structure of doctrines, ideas, and beliefs remained not only unchanged but ossified, an ossification perpetuated through the educational system that came into being in about the twelfth century. While law and theology, therefore, did not offer to creative minds a great scope for the exercise of talents, Sufism did, and it has been rightly said that in the later medieval centuries, Sufism afforded a congenial home for geniuses with creative minds and spirits. Sufism, however, inculcated passivity among its adherents. With law and theology having become stagnant and petrified from about the thirteenth–fourteenth centuries C.E., the Muslim community seemed to languish, both intellectually and morally.

In the eighteenth century, a reaction began against this state of affairs. One reaction, emerging in the Arabian peninsula and in certain other African and Asian countries, including India, is known as "Islamic fundamentalism." Its advocates attributed the stagnation of Islamic spiritual and moral life to Muslims' deviation, during the medieval centuries, from the norms set by the Qur'an and the Sunna of the Prophet. Their call to "go back to the Qur'an and the Sunna of the Prophet" did good in putting before Muslims afresh the ideals of pristine Islam, but a great deal of harm also followed, particularly in the intellectual sphere. In their bid to debunk the medieval intellectual heritage of Islam as well as its spiritual heritage in order to go back to the sources, the representatives of these movements oversimplified the educational curricula, de-emphasizing the heritage of the medieval disciplines of learning. These disciplines of learning, although they had become petrified, had nevertheless developed a rich heritage, and by abandoning this heritage, the leaders of the new fundamentalist or revivalist movements impoverished the intellectual life of their followers. Among these movements, the most influential was the Wahhābī movement of peninsular Arabia, which established its puritanical ideology in a new state thenceforward known as Saudi Arabia. The fortunes of such fundamentalist movements, of course, varied in different countries, but basic to them all was a bid to assume political power and to bring about rigorous reform through state machinery.

In some lands of Islam, however, besides the simple fundamentalist reaction, a second alternative arose because of the introduction of modern education along Western lines. In Turkey, Egypt, and the Indian Subcontinent, a modern educational system was established parallel to the traditional *madrasa* education. Out of the confrontation between the two educations grew the phenomenon known as "Islamic modernism." Brilliant and seminal intellectuals, who attempted on the one hand the acculturation of the new modern spirit with the traditionalist Islamic heritage and on the other the reform and modernization of traditionalism, grew up in all these lands. These modernists, curiously, took their stand on the heritage of the fundamentalist movements themselves. They espoused the basic idea of the fundamentalists that Muslims had in various spheres of life deviated from the original norms of Islam, but whereas the fundamentalists' panacea was simply to go back to the pristine monotheism of Islam, the modernist reformers sought to give a new content to Islam in various areas, political, social, legal, and educational. They argued, for example, that in the political sphere, the Qur'an had left for Muslims a legacy of "rule on the basis of mutual consultation" (*shūrā*), which is a democratic process (Qur'an 42, 38). The Muslims themselves, in medieval times, had deviated from this democratic norm and acquiesced in the semiautocratic rule of sultans and amirs. The modernists therefore called for the reintroduction of democracy in Islam. Similarly they argued that the Qur'an had given a great many rights to women but that these rights had been steadily encroached upon in medieval times. Here, again, they called for social reform and restoration of the rights of women, including their education. The modernists also brought about legal reform in various spheres of life; the only area practically untouched until the late 1950s was the area of family law, and changes there have been brought about even to the present. As a result of the activity of the modernists, constitutional governments were inducted in many Muslim countries, legal reform was begun, women's rights were legislated, and by the early decades of this century, it seemed that Islam had taken to the modern path. By this is meant not necessarily the modern *Western* path, for most Muslim modernists, while espousing some key Western ideals along with scientific education, severely criticized the deteriorating moral standards of Western societies.

However, by the 1920s, a neofundamentalist reaction against these modernizing trends appeared. All over the Muslim world, organized movements arose to reassert the medieval Islamic institutions and general way of life against the modernist reforms. While the main reason behind these neo-fundamentalist phenomena was the intense anti-Western feeling generated by Western European colonialism, their virulence also attacked the mod-dernist thought within Islam itself. As a consequence, at the present, we are witnessing the rise of neorevivalists like Khomeini in Iran and Zia Ul-Haq in Pakistan and the new rise of the Muslim Brotherhood and several extremist splinter groups of that movement in Egypt and elsewhere; we also see strong revivalist phenomena in Turkey, Malaysia, and Indonesia. The shared characteristic of these neorevivalists is that they are practically totally unclear about their goals. By and large, they oppose democracy but they do not know what to put in its place, for they are also against personal rule; they are against the emancipation and public role of women, but they do not know of any constructive alternative goals for women to follow. They certainly espouse modern science and, particularly, modern technology—the single item in the modern Muslim legacy that they consider good. Nevertheless, in practice, they do not assign to science and technology any significant priority. The current phenomenon is, at its roots, negative; some new solution on Muslim modernist lines is requisite to end this unthinking revivalist phenomenon, but it must avoid the traps of ethical deterioration into which the West seems to have fallen at present.

For readers interested in knowing more about Islam, the following are recommended, in order of comprehensiveness: H. A. R. Gibb's *Mohammedanism: An Historical Survey* (Oxford: Oxford University Press, 1951); Fazlur Rahman's *Islam*, 2d ed. (Chicago: University of Chicago Press, 1979); and Marshall G. Hodgson's *Venture of Islam: Conscience and History in a World Civilization*, 3 vols. (Chicago: University of Chicago Press, 1974).

·1·

Wellness and Illness in the Islamic World View

In order to be able to appreciate the value system of Islam, it is essential to know something of its basic beliefs and outlook on life. This is perhaps more true of Islam than any other religion because, from the very beginning, Islam has had a very moral and practical attitude toward life and has exhibited relatively little enthusiasm for metaphysical speculation. The spiritual-cultural background from which it arose was the same as that of Syriac Christianity, which, with its moral élan and distrust of speculation, can be sharply distinguished from the Greek and Roman versions of Christianity, characterized respectively by a speculative and a legal outlook. Recent scholarship has shown beyond any doubt that the accounts of Judaism and Christianity presented in the Qur'an have Syriac Christianity as their background. Later in Islam many speculative theological, philosophical, and mystical systems were constructed which have profoundly influenced the Islamic world view, but they were never able to supplant this practical moral trend. For this reason, the explicit theological content of the Qur'an is minimal, but by the same token, whatever theology there is, is strictly linked to action. Its understanding is crucial to an adequate understanding of the behaviorial attitudes inculcated by the Qur'an.[1]

GOD, NATURE, AND HUMANKIND

The central aim of the Qur'an is to influence and provide guidance for human conduct. Although the nature per se of God is not discussed, God nevertheless stands at the very basis of the Qur'an's entire doctrinal teaching: without God nothing can exist, let alone work. He constitutes the very integrity of every existent, particularly of humankind, both individually and socially. God alone is infinite and original being; all else is created by him and necessarily suffers from finitude. Hence the persistent Qur'anic condemnations of "worshiping other than God" or "assigning partners to God." The four most fundamental relational qualities of God, particularly vis-à-vis humans, are creation, sustenance, guidance, and judgment. All these constitute a chain that is, for the Qur'an, logically interconnected, and this whole represents the infinite mercy of God. The creation of the universe is itself God's primordial mercy, for in and by itself the universe has no warrant to exist. There could well have been a pure emptiness of nothing rather than this actual plenitude of being, but for the unbounded mercy of God.

Nature is therefore the handiwork of God and points beyond itself to him. It works by laws that have been inlaid in it by God. Whenever God creates something, it falls into a pattern with the rest, resulting in cosmos rather than in chaos. Nature is one huge, firm, and well-knit machine: there are in it no gaps, no ruptures, no dislocations. Hence nature is autonomous, not autocratic, because it did not bring itself into being. It is interesting to note the development in the Qur'an of the doctrine of miracles. It accepted from the earlier Semitic religious traditions the stories of the miracles performed by Abraham, Moses, Jesus, and other biblical figures, although it insisted that the miracles were not produced by prophets but by God at the prophets' hands. But when his Meccan opponents pressed Muhammad for miracles, the Qur'an's answer was that it itself was miraculous and that no human agency could produce another Qur'an. As for supernatural miracles, these had been given to earlier prophets, it is true, but they were never effective against disbelievers, so there would be no more of them (Qur'an 17, 59).

Nature has been created by God for humankind to exploit and use for its good purposes. Numerous verses in the Qur'an proclaim that God has "made subservient the heaven and the earth and whatever is in them to humankind" (31, 20; cf. 2, 29; 45, 12). Human beings alone were created "to serve God" and none else, including "man's subjective whims" (*al-ahwā'*). Therefore, while nature is subservient to them, humans must not "get lost" in nature so that they lose both God and self. These verses of the Qur'an have been heavily underlined by modern Muslim reformers since the middle of the last century in order to reawaken Muslims' interest in science after its eclipse among them for centuries.

Although for the Qur'an humans are the noblest of all creatures, they can nevertheless come down "to the lowest of the low" (95, 4ff.) unless they redeem themselves through faith and good works. The most fundamental weakness of humans, for the Qur'an, is their pettiness, narrow-mindedness, and selfishness. Even their idolatry directly springs from pettiness of mind, for idol-worship presupposes the closure of one's mind to the infinitude of transcendence. It is the awareness of transcendence (which is, in essence, equivalent to God-consciousness) that creates the necessary space for the "rise" of humankind to God and for its necessary progress; otherwise, people become locked in stagnation and disintegrate. The answer to this vicious ailment of pettiness and narrowness is to "transcend" oneself by self-giving to others. The Qur'an tells us that it is Satan who whispers in people's minds that by giving to others, by investing in the poor segments of society, they will become proportionately impoverished; God, on the contrary, "promises forgiveness and prosperity" for such social investment (2, 260ff.). It seems certain, in view of the polytheism of the pagan Meccans and the great socioeconomic disparity between the rich and the poor and the general social irresponsibility in that society, that the extraordinary Qur'anic emphases on monotheism on the one hand and socioeconomic justice and egalitarianism on the other are organically linked—the Qur'an seems to proclaim "one God, one humanity."

Interestingly, three key terms in the Qur'an relate to human conduct, all of which mean "to be safe," "to be integral and sound." The first term is *īmān*, which means "faith," but its root (*a m n*) means "to be at peace," "to be safe," "not to be exposed to danger." The idea is that faith bestows safety and peace. The second term, *islām*, comes from the root *s l m*, which means "to be safe," "to be whole and integral," "not to disintegrate." The idea is that by accepting the law of God and "surrendering" to it, one avoids disintegration. The third fundamental concept is *taqwā*, which is usually translated as "piety" or "fear of God" but whose root (*w q y*) means to "protect from getting lost or wasted" and "to guard against peril." This constellation of basic terms clearly brings home the most important notion of Islam about humankind (although the Qur'an also applies the term *islām* to the entire nature insofar as it obeys God's law and thus preserves itself), concerning attitude (belief) and behavior: people can and ought to avoid moral and physical peril, conform to the law of God for persons (as nature obeys its own laws), and thus save themselves individually and collectively *from* perdition and *for* developing their vast potentialities for "doing service to God," that is, obeying God's (moral) law. This "development" is squarely based on human performance, individual and collective. It is in this connection that the Qur'an repeatedly emphasizes the "weighing of deeds." The future of every individual insofar as the Last Judgment is concerned, or the fate of every society insofar as history is concerned, depends essentially on the quality of their performance, which constitutes its "weight." The ideal of judgment, whether upon individuals or upon societies, is rationalized on the basis of the real worth of their performance, for often a deed appears "weighty" to the doer but objectively and ultimately worthless and even harmful. This true worth can be brought out only in the long view, at the "end" (*ākhira*), because the short-run vision of people is more often than not blurred; they take certain deeds to be prodigious which turn out to be no more than "motes scattered around" with no real substance or worth.

This deep self-deception, which constitutes perhaps the greatest failing of human nature, is, of course, also rooted in narrow-mindedness and myopic vision. The only cure for it is *taqwā*, which is cultivated by constant self-examination until an inner torch sparks out whereby one can X-ray oneself, so to speak, and "guard against peril." A person who has so morally cultivated himself or herself need not fear the Last Judgment, for the function of the judgment, after all, is to excavate the self from this "grave-within-grave" of self-deception (arising from all myopic interests—personal, family, or national interests, or indeed any group interests) and enable a person to see himself or herself in his nakedness. "In that hour [of truth], a man shall flee from his brother, his mother and father, and his own sons—for every one that day will have his own preoccupation" (80, 32–37). The "next creation," or the "next form or level of creation," then, will essentially depend upon human performance on earth, although the Qur'an frequently emphasizes God's grace and mercy, his pardon and forgiveness in this connection. Thus the new form or level of creation will, according to the Qur'an, entail a rearrangement of the factors and forces, direction and purposes of life, although the afterlife is also often portrayed in rather static terms of the joys of paradise and tortures of hell. What is crucial in all this is the quality of human performance.

Both the relation of faith and reason in the Qur'an and the related problem of divine determination and human free will have serious consequences for Islam's practical outlook on life. Faith in God is an absolute necessity, for without this faith human values become distorted; the entire human conduct, both individual and collective, becomes mechanical and is thrown out of perspective. But faith is not something irrational; it is, indeed, in a sense generative of its own reason although in itself it is not reason but a commitment. Still, it is not generated by any *formal* or theological reasoning: it arises, rather, out of observing a certain empirical evidence in a certain way, just as a spark arises when a match is struck in a certain way. The evidence is the *empirical fact of being*, and faith is the awareness that this universe, this plenitude of being, points to a certain ground upon which it must rest.

This whole discussion of faith in God may at first appear irrelevant to what follows in this monograph. It may be held (and in the modern world it is often held) that generally people are born with an instinct of compassion and because of this they like to help those in disease and distress. Against this, others would say that it is God who has implanted this instinct and that the exercise of this instinct of mercy or pity fulfills God's natural command. This raises the question of the source of moral values: is it nature without God or is it nature as ordained by God? No Muslims have held to the first view except for a few deists or quasi-deists, but the second view was held by the Mu'tazilite school (the rationalist school of theology begun in the eighth century C.E.), who insisted that one could discover what is good and what is evil by the natural reason that God had put in humans, even unaided by revelation. Islamic orthodoxy, however, by way of reaction against the Mu'tazilites, came to the view that God dictated what was good and what was evil through a series of revelations from Adam to Muhammad and that natural reason per se never yields genuine and decisive moral imperatives but only inspires conduct in conformity with one's self-interest. It therefore held that if one saves a person's life through sheer satisfaction gained by indulging one's instinct of mercy, it cannot properly be called a moral act unless it takes revelation into account. Neither of these opinions expresses the Qur'an's view, which posits an intimate and positive connection between reason and revelation (and such one-sided theological developments are not uncommon in religious traditions), but they do underline the importance of the nature and source of moral values and have a fundamental bearing on the formation of human attitudes from which human conduct flows.

A related problem is that of free will. The Qur'an's aim is essentially to unleash and maximize human moral energy, so it cannot deny the potency of either humankind or God. From its point of view, God, nature, and human beings are all effective causational principles, each at a different level. Clouds *cause* rains, God *brings* rains particularly for human benefit, while humans *use* rains and other natural resources for their good ends. The Qur'an therefore *cannot* accept a contradiction between natural causation and human free will or between divine causation and human free will. None of these operates at the expense of the other two. Divine activity is, of course, over-arching and *operates through* natural and human activity as their meaning or *telos*, without which both of them would become perverted, delinquent, and self-wasting. Determinism and free will, potency and impotency, hope and fear are, in the human case, not contradictions but rather God-given tensions *within* whose framework people must work; should they violate either side of the tension and think themselves to be either omnipotent or impotent, they fall into a Satanic condition that the Qur'an calls *kufr*, a term usually understood to mean "disbelief" or "rejection of truth" but which basically means total privation of moral energy. When theological speculation arose in Islam in the eighth century C.E., these categories of tensions were rendered mutually exclusive. The Mu'tazilite school solved the problem by denying God's activity in the sphere of human free will and confining it to the field of nature; this they found necessary in order to preserve human responsibility and divine justice. The Ash'arite (orthodox) reaction that came in the tenth century denied any power to humans or real efficacy to human will in the interest of saving God's omnipotence. This divine omnipotence also required, in their view, that nature of itself be ineffective: they denied causation, autonomous natural laws (which they reformulated as *habits* of God), and continuity and therefore affirmed atomicity of both time and space.

It was, nevertheless, impossible to give up the idea of causation at the practical level, notwithstanding theological formulations. Undoubtedly these formulations were further bolstered by the growth of speculative Sufism (Islamic mysticism), which overwhelmed the Muslim world particularly from the fourteenth to the eighteenth century and which strongly inculcated the idea of God as the only cause of all events. Despite this powerful coalition of orthodox theology and Sufi spirituality, however, no peasant ever believed that God would grow his crops whether or not he sowed the seeds or watered his crops. And no doctor (indeed, few patients) could believe that medical treatment was futile because it was God who did or did not do the healing. The general attitude that finally came to settle among Muslims, whether learned or not, was that it is God who produces all events in nature and in persons, but that he does not do so without certain objective conditions. Humans are charged with producing and manipulating these conditions and interfering in nature in certain ways, but it is God who causes the result.

It is obvious, though, that this position is itself capable of change of emphasis. On one extreme, a small minority gives the strongest emphasis to natural causation; on the other, an infinitesimal minority practically discounts natural causation, while the vast majority holds or assumes the position that God acts *on the basis* of natural causes. The Qur'an's position appears to be that God acts *through* natural causation and human volition to further his purposes.

THE SOCIAL OUTLOOK OF THE QUR'AN

At the individual level the Qur'an sought to inculcate piety, or *taqwā*; at the social level it aimed at creating a sociopolitical order on a viable ethical basis. There was supposed to be an intimate relationship between the two sides: although the societal side assumed personal *taqwā* (without which it would and did become an instrument of tyranny), *taqwā* itself was expected to express itself in the social dimension, without which it could, and indeed often did, become a negative, other-worldly spirituality, particularly in certain forms of Sufism. This sociopolitical activity the Qur'an calls "reforming the earth and removing corruption therefrom."

The first principle of reform is the essential egalitarianism of humankind. This principle, however, developed in tension with that of the solidarity of the Muslim community, which was ironically generated by the same belief in one universal God and one indivisible humanity: the community worked on behalf of God. In any case, the task of this community was defined as "commanding good and forbidding evil with faith in God" (2, 142; 3, 110). The community was, however, given no unconditional assurance of success or salvation unless it came up to its task (47, 35)—the Qur'an had already accused other communities of having taken God for granted and laying proprietary claims to his guidance. Despite this, partly through external rivalry with other religious communities but largely through its internal dynamics of religious development—the need for the authority of the community's consensus (*ijmāʿ*)—the community did come to claim infallibility for itself, in the teeth of the Qur'an, and sometime in the ninth century these words came to be attributed to the Prophet Muhammad: "My community shall never agree on an error."

Notwithstanding these quasi-exclusivist claims, however, Muslims were able to be open to non-Muslim communities and peoples at a cultural level. Indeed, Islamic civilization was the first international civilization on an almost global scale involving people of different faiths, races, and nationalities. As such, it was a genuine precursor of modern Western civilization, which, however, became international after having become secular. Of the three great Western religions, Islam is the least race- and color-conscious. Islam itself, of course, comprised Arabs, Turks, Persians, Indians, Malaysians, Indonesians, blacks, and Berbers, who all constituted a single Muslim community with its center of gravity at Mecca. But in Baghdad and particularly in Spain a multifaith culture came into being under Muslim aegis. Baghdad became an important center of interfaith discussions and debates which were mostly held in private but whose atmosphere, judging from the accounts, was extraordinarily liberal. In one such gathering, for example, we are told that when a Muslim quoted from the Qur'an, one participant replied, "Please do not quote the Qur'an in this meeting because many of us do not believe in it, and if we had believed in it, there would have been no point in having this meeting."[2] Again in eleventh-century Baghdad, the philosopher and doctor Abu'l-Barakāt ibn Malkā attained his highest office as physician at the caliphal court as a Jew and became Muslim only late in his life. In Spain, Muslims, Christians, and Jews systematically collaborated in the fields of philosophy, medicine, and science, even in literature, to produce a brilliant multifaith civilization for the first time in human history. Jewish scholars normally wrote their philosophy and science in Arabic and their theology in Hebrew as did Moses Maimonides (d. 1204), who also wrote his commentaries on the Ten Commandments and the Mishnah in Arabic. Maimonides finally settled in Cairo as the personal physician to Saladin (Ṣalāḥ al-Dīn al-Ayyūbī), the famous adversary of the crusader Richard the Lion-Hearted.

In medicine the number of non-Muslims—Christians and Jews but also Zoroastrians and Hindus—is large indeed, proportionate to their population in the Middle Eastern Muslim lands. From Greece Muslims got scientific, medical, and philosophical works which they translated with great zest from Greek into Arabic (often via Syriac)—but not Greek religion and literature. Some scientific and medical works were also translated from Sanskrit. In the fields of philosophy and science the contributions of non-Muslims became both less numerous and generally less important than those of Muslims over time, but in medicine Christians and Jews continued to play a prominent role alongside Muslims both in the production of first-rate works and in medical practice. The explanation seems to lie in the fact that with medicine's being a practical art of fundamental importance, many more medical experts were needed than scientists and philosophers and also, as we shall see later when we speak of the Prophetic Medicine literature, Muslims had bestowed on the art of healing exceptionally high religious value and priority.

In summary, so far as a person's situation vis-à-vis God, nature, and fellow humans is concerned, Islam offers a cohesive outlook on life, at the center of which stands human well-being. The three most fundamental religious concepts in Islam—all basic to the teaching of the Qur'an itself—mean safety, wholeness, and integrality as opposed to danger, fragmentation, and destruction through disintegration. It is equally important to note that the Qur'an describes the function of genuine faith in God as saving man from disintegration and cementing his personality: "Be not like those who forgot God and [eventually] God caused them to forget themselves" (59, 19). Finally, the Qur'an reiterates that all wrong a person does to others is done in a far more fundamental and ultimate sense against the subject himself or herself, and, further, that that is true both of individuals and societies. Conversely, all good done to others reflects in turn on the personality of the agent.

THE SOURCES

The Qur'an

When we talk of wellness and illness in the present work, we obviously mean *human* conditions. All creatures with some form of life have, of course, wellness and illness (and some would say that even inorganic matter has its sound and unsound states). Health and unhealth or wholesomeness and unwholesomeness are universal conditions wherever life in any form is found, and, further, to avoid or cure disease is also as much a natural law as, say, the law of gravity.

When we consider life at the human level, however, we are faced with an infinitely complex situation. With the emergence of life also arises the instinct of pugnacity. The operations of this instinct cannot be adequately explained by an appeal to the instinct of survival and the law of survival of the fittest. It appears to be an independent instinct. When this instinct is conjoined with the phenomenon that as life ascends the scale of evolution, the gap between potentialities and their actual realization among the members of the same species increases, domination of some members over others becomes a law. It reaches its pinnacle in humankind. Aristotle committed the original sin when he defined humans as "rational animals": they are certainly animals who can use reason when they like, mainly to further animal goals. Whereas humans are raised and ennobled by reason, when this reason is put at the disposal of animality, they become worse than animals, and to this the Qur'an is pointing when it says: "We created man in the best of molds but then we sent him down to be the lowest of the low, except those who believe and do good deeds . . ." (95, 4–5).

This verse might also be interpreted to refer to the Fall of Adam and Eve from the Garden of Eden into temporal life on earth. There are, of course, references in the Qur'an to the state of bliss in which Adam and Eve were, whence they fell. But the Qur'an does not represent this episode as such a radical moral rupture as did Christianity. It merely says that Adam and Eve were "misled" by the Devil (*Iblis*) into tasting the tree of life, whereby they lost their innocence, but then they were reconciled to God (2, 36–38).

The Qur'an also never refers to that state of bliss as the Garden of Eden; the Garden of Eden is still to come for those "who believe and do good deeds." The "best of molds" therefore appears to refer to the ideal (that is, real) nature of humans *in this world* whence they fall and "gravitate down to the earth," as the Qur'an (7, 175) puts it, describing the fall of a prophet from the height of divine bliss into the clutches of Satan.

No matter how high a person's moral and spiritual station, then, he or she cannot take it for granted and feel immune; one has always *to try* not to fall but to climb up. On the other hand, even though the Qur'an constantly talks about how God renders some people "deaf" to truth, "seals up" their hearts, and makes their "eyes blind" so they cannot see, there is nevertheless no point of no return, for always open is the door of "return" or repentance (*tauba*), which can turn evil personalities upside down and inside out and make them into saints. One thing is certain: that Satan came into being along with humankind, for before Adam there was no Satan, according to the Qur'an. In the story of Adam's creation the Qur'an (2, 30ff.) tells us that when God made his decision known to angels ("I am going to place on the earth my vicegerent"), the angels asked with a sense of shock, "Are you going to place therein a being who will sow corruption therein and shed blood, while we sing your praises and glorify your holiness?" In reply God apparently did not deny the angels' charges against humankind but said, "I know that which you know not." He then made known to Adam through a creative capacity for knowledge "all the names." When he asked the angels if they knew the names of things, they said they only knew things he had told them and nothing more. When Adam was able to name things, God ordered angels to honor Adam by prostrating before him for his creative knowledge. They all did so except one being who became Satan for his disobedience and turned into the eternal enemy of humankind.

In this story, God's making known to Adam all names has been interpreted as bestowing upon him the capacity for creative knowledge; otherwise God would be cheating angels and also Adam's knowledge would be mechanical rather than creative. In their ability for creative knowledge, then, human beings outstrip all creatures. Further, in the whole of creation, humans alone are endowed with free choice, which neither nature nor angels possess. This is what the Qur'anic statement in 33, 77 appears to refer to: "We offered the trust to the heavens and the earth and the mountains, but they refused to accept it and were afraid of it, but man bore it—man is indeed a tyrant over himself and foolhardy." This verse strongly implies that humankind has not made much right use of its freedom. This is confirmed by another verse: "Nay, humans have *not yet* fulfilled what

God had commanded them through their primordial moral nature" (80, 23).

Thus, whereas people possess an unrivaled capacity for producing new knowledge, it is in the moral sphere that their persistent failure appears. The task of the Qur'an is to help them in this sphere, which is why it calls itself "guidance for humankind." It is, of course, not a book of science or medicine, but it does proffer itself as the "restorer of health," which has been taken by Muslims to mean that its guidance leads to both spiritual (and psychological) and physical health. The same conclusion also follows from the basic Qur'anic concepts of safety, completeness, and integrality, for with a physically sick condition or disposition a person can obviously not be whole. When one Muslim meets another the salutation is *salām*, "peace and wholeness be with you." Indeed, the Qur'an declares God's function vis-à-vis humankind to be the preservation of human integrity which disappears both from individual and collective life with the removal of God from human consciousness: "O you who believe! be conscious of God and let a person see well what he or she sends forth for the morrow—constantly be God-conscious, for God is aware of what you do. And be not like those who forgot God and [eventually] God caused them to forget themselves—these are the unrighteous ones" (59, 18–19).

The Qur'an does not appear to subscribe to the doctrine of a radical mind-body dualism. It does not hold that a heavenly soul and an earthly body somehow come together in an uneasy union or bond whence the soul seeks release as soon as possible. The term *nafs*, which occurs so frequently in the Qur'an and is translated into English as "soul," actually means "person" or else is a reflective pronoun meaning "itself," "himself," "herself," and so on, and not "soul," a concept that does not seem to occur in the Qur'an. A human being, for the Qur'an, is a single organism functioning in a certain fashion. A person is not just the outer body, the "physical frame," but includes an inner person which may be called "mind"; together they form one organized unit. For this reason it holds forth belief in the *revival* of the dead. Later when through the legacy of Greek philosophy the idea of a radical mind-body dualism came into Islam, belief arose in *survivalism* of the soul at death and the destruction forever of the body. But the belief did not affect orthodox doctrine, although Muslim philosophers and many Sufis held to it. From this point of view also, the Qur'an could not have embraced a notion of the soul as being healthy and the body being sick or vice versa. Hence it is said of Saul, for example, "We gave him amplitude in body and in knowledge" (2, 246).

A little reflection shows that human life can be lived correctly and productively only if humankind works within the framework of certain given tensions. Certainly, the Qur'an appears to uphold such a framework. Free will and determinism constitute one of these tensions: humans, at their own level, are certainly free agents, and denial of this freedom would undercut the entire teaching of the Qur'an as an invitation to goodness. The Qur'an explicitly states this in numerous places. But at the same time it asserts an all-embracing higher will, that of God. Humans must work within this frame of human freedom and divine omnipotence. Similarly, they are not omniscient but neither are they ignorant, and they can always go on expanding areas of knowledge. Again, they must work within the perspective of hope, on the one hand, which is the moral basis of human endeavor (but without thinking humanity to be "the measure of all things") and of despair and hopelessness on the other. Working consciously within these tensions unleashes human moral energy to the maximum, which is undoubtedly the aim of the Qur'an. To violate either side of these tensions results in a total loss of moral energy. Satan himself exemplifies this: his pride first led him to disobey God's command to honor Adam, but after he fell, his utter hopelessness that his moral personality could be reconstituted and redeemed made him a professional evilmonger.

Taqwā, or sense of responsibility, in fact, cannot be maintained unless one synthesizes these contradictory poles in one's conduct. This is what the Qur'an calls the "straight path," the "upright religion," and this is also why it characterizes the Muslim community as the "median community" which was expected to synthesize extremes rather than negate them. For by negating the polarities, human conduct becomes abstract and loses its grip on concrete life. When the Qur'an called Muslims the median community, it most probably meant its mediating role between what it perceived to be the particularism of Judaism and the excessively accommodating attitude of Christianity. But, by analogical extension, this mediation can be between any two perceived extremes, for example, between capitalism and extreme socialism or between rigid conservatism and reckless change.

The Tradition (Ḥadīth)

The Ḥadīth, which is the corpus of traditions upon which the life of the Muslim community is largely based and its institutions rationalized, claims to represent the Prophet's extra-Qur'anic precepts and examples.[3] In reality, however, it largely represents the opinions of the early generations of Muslims and can be taken as a vast commentary by these generations upon the Qur'an and the performance of the Prophet. Reasonableness would require that not the entirety of this corpus be apocryphal, for the Prophet had obviously given precepts, set examples (*sunna*), decided cases, and made policies outside the Qur'an. It would, however, be a herculean task to examine this massive material from the perspective of historical criticism, and, until the present, historical criticism of the tradition has not been able to find its way among Muslims who fear that should Ḥadīth collapse, the entire fabric of traditional law and institutions in Islam would collapse. But as modern scholarly techniques of research, analysis, and criticism spread among Muslims, such historical criticism of Ḥadīth is sure to get underway. Signs of uneasiness about the issue are already visible among the more advanced modern educated circles.

Our task here is not to essay such a critique of Ḥadīth but to look at its contribution to our understanding of well-being. Certainly it has introduced new elements into this field, modifying, sometimes quite seriously, the teaching of the Qur'an and bringing new and often contradictory factors to bear upon problems of human concern. The most fundamental change it wrought or justified stems from its general advocacy of pacifism, acceptance of the status quo, and discouraging of activism. This is true of both Sunni and Shi'a Ḥadīth, although there also exists much idealism in Shi'ism—arising from the concept of martyrdom connected with the bloody death of Ḥusain, as discussed above in the historical introduction.

As a result of the early schismatic developments outlined above, Sunni (and to a large extent Shi'a) Islam advocated the status quo and conformism in both the religious and the political domains and was content with minimal knowledge of Islam and its practice on the part of an average Muslim. This is expressed through several Ḥadīths like the following:

> The Prophet one day said to Abū Dharr al-Ghifārī [one of his companions —earlier this report is attributed to another companion Abu'l-Dardā'], "O Abū Dharr! a person who professes 'there is no God but Allah' goes to paradise." "Even though he should commit adultery and theft?" asked the companion, and the Prophet replied, "Yes, even if he should commit adultery and theft." The companion repeated the question twice and each time received the same answer, even more emphatically.[4]

Similarly, abundant Ḥadīth is available exhorting the faithful against political rebellion and inculcating almost unconditional acceptance of the status quo. Any person who reads the Qur'an carefully will be struck by its preoccupation with "good works," words which appear invariably after "belief"; "Those who believe and do good works" is reiterated untiringly. Indeed in two passages (2, 62; 5, 69) the Qur'an promises God's favors and salvation to whosoever "believe in God and the Last Day and do good works" from among Muslims, Jews, Christians, and Sabians (a religious community whose identity is not ascertainable but possibly a Syrian community with a Gnostic-Neoplatonic belief system) without mentioning belief in the messengership of the Prophet Muhammad—so intent is the Qur'an on good works. The Ḥadīth in question is therefore a Murji'a reaction to the Khārijite stand, adopted later by both Sunnis and the Shi'a. This produced the Islamic counterpart of the Christian doctrine of justification by faith. This Irjā' mentality was further accentuated by the doctrine of intercession: the belief that all prophets, and especially Muhammad, will successfully intercede on behalf of the sinners of their communities. This belief was opposed by the Khārijites and the Mu'tazilite school of rationalist theology but was later universally accepted by Muslims, despite the Qur'an's emphasis on hope for sinners which rests squarely on God's unlimited mercy and forgiveness and which appears to deny intercession.

The Qur'an seeks to inculcate a healthy, middle-of-the-road attitude on morality. While its warnings of punishment are very stark, so is its hope in God's compassion and forgiveness. While its call to goodness is unfailing, it seeks to avoid moral frenzy and panic: "If you avoid the grave sins that are prohibited to you, we shall obliterate [the effects] of occasional and smaller lapses" (9, 31); "And those are [true believers] who avoid major evils and obscenities, and when they are under the influence of anger, they exercise forgiveness" (42, 37); "Those are [true believers] who avoid major evils and obscenities, except [occasionally] coming to their brink" (53, 32). A good work earns its reward ten times over, while an evil deed draws out an equivalent response (6, 16)—that is, if it is not forgiven.

To their paraphernalia of Irjā', the Sunni traditions added yet another powerful factor. The Sunni tradition and Sunni theology now went all the way in negating human will and power in order to establish God's power and will. Neither humans nor anything else in nature, according to the Ash'arites—advocates of the Sunni doctrine that reigned supreme for a thousand years—has any inherent power to act. Such power is created in people (or anything else) when they actually act and is then withdrawn by God. Extreme divine determinism is unabashedly expressed in a tradition attributed to the Prophet and recorded in all major Sunni Ḥadīth works: "When God created all human souls in pre-eternity, he took some of them in his right hand and threw them, saying, 'Unto paradise you go, and little do I care' and others he took in his left hand and threw them, saying, 'Unto hell you go, and little do I care.'"[5] The Shi'a Ḥadīth, as it developed on this issue, is much more sophisticated. Although the earliest Shi'a doctrine is crudely materialistic, it became increasingly refined beginning with the tenth century C.E., as it progressively came under the influence of the

Mu'tazilite school of theology. Its first formulation of the new stance was "Man is neither entirely free nor wholly predetermined but is somewhere between the two."[6] Later, however, beginning with the thirteenth century, it became an unconditional champion of human free will and some Shi'a theologians went so far as to describe God as "determined" by human will. It seems the Shi'a were consciously putting the Sunnis in their place!

The Irjā' movement in Islam had been initially helped by the Umayyad ruling dynasty, and indeed the entire Khārijite-Irjā'ist phenomenon originated from a political background. This had disastrous effects on subsequent political theory in Islam. The fear of Khārijite rebellionism led Muslims almost to an apotheosis of pacifism and political conformism; any measure that might lead to disunity and dissension within the community was religiously tabooed. Although in the first two and a half centuries or so the political jurists did insist on high qualifications for a caliph and looked as well at his personal qualities, later these were drastically modified when the caliph began to rule through a team of advisors or viziers and a bureaucratic structure. Indeed, he came to be declared "God's shadow on earth" under inspiration from the ancient Iranian ideal of the divine king. Effective usurpation of power through force came to be unceremoniously legitimized.

It is clear that these Irjā'ist developments inevitably had the effect of lowering the moral energy level of Muslims in responding to the demands of the Qur'an. Yet two factors relieved the grimness of this situation considerably. First, the Sharī'a, the Sacred Law, set limits on the ruler's exercise of power: a tyrant in the real sense of the term could not arise in Islam, because no ruler could gravely violate the divine law with much hope of impunity. Second, arising ironically out of Irjā'ism itself, a strong sense of the community prevailed, for the basic raison d'être of Irjā'ism was to keep the community intact even at the relative expense of the intensity of the moral sense. While in the Qur'an's ideal vision, moral intensity was to generate a community of the faithful which would embody and implement it, a pragmatic moral sense was effectively generated by the idea of the community itself which, as noted before, in brazen opposition to the Qur'an was declared infallible. This sense of the community and of a social ethic—even though far removed from the Qur'anic vision—directly inspired undertaking of works of social weal, including medical services.

Sufism

To a large extent in conscious distinction from, and in some cases even in conscious opposition to, the legal-theological formulation of Islam at the hands of Islamic orthodoxy, there developed its spiritual expression in mystical form known as Sufism.[7] One prominent feature of Sufi spirituality was the great distrust, shared by many of its representatives, of formal learning and logical reason. In contradistinction to intellectual activity, they emphasized intuitive understanding and certainty. Stories abound of Sufi adepts who were accomplished scholars but who, when they entered upon the Way, threw away all their books. Al-Ghazālī tells us in his spiritual autobiography, *The Rescuer from the Stray Path*, of his disenchantment with formal theology (*kalām*) of which he was a professor at the Niẓāmīya College at Baghdad, how he resigned his post in a spiritual crisis, studied philosophy and wrote his famous *Incoherence of the Philosophers*, and eventually found repose in Sufism and the "inner meaning of the Sacred Law."[8] According to an anecdote connected with his conversion, al-Ghazālī was traveling with a caravan when it was attacked and robbed by a gang of highway men. Al-Ghazālī, whose books were also taken by robbers, went to their chief and asked him to return the books because "they are of no use to you." "Of what use are they to *you*?" retorted the chief of the robbers. "They contain knowledge which I study," replied al-Ghazālī. "Oh!" exclaimed the chief of the robbers sarcastically, "So your knowledge is in books and now that your books are gone you have no knowledge, poor man!" and returned the books. This traumatic event is said to have sent al-Ghazālī into his spiritual crisis.[9] There are also many accounts of highly learned scholars sitting at the feet of semi-literate and even totally illiterate Sufi shaikhs to get spiritual enlightenment.

However, although the phenomenon described above was not uncommon, in later medieval centuries, particularly when the 'Ulama began to enroll in Sufi orders, it was quite usual for the learned Sufi shaikh to teach orthodox disciplines of theology, law, and Qur'an exegesis in the morning in the mosque and lead spiritual sessions and exercises in the evening in his spiritual precinct or lodge (called *zāwiya* in Arabic, *tekke* in Turkish, and *khānqāh* in Iran and the Subcontinent). From the earliest times had arisen a movement, more or less successful, to keep the potentially riotous Sufi expressions of religion within check and produce an orthodox version of it. But on its outskirts always lay a vast area of unregulated spirituality in constant tension with orthodox Islam.

The second most important feature of Sufism was its turning of Muslims' gaze inward and away from the community of Islam. This does not mean that Sufis were disconnected from society; on the contrary, they did a great deal of social service, catered for the poor in their hospices, and attended to the sick in their own way by prayers and amulets. Being near the masses, as distinguished from the elitist Islam of the 'Ulama, they were intermediaries between the masses and the governments and frequently rose to rebel in the cause of justice and to remove public distress when this became intolerable. Several of them rose in defense of Islam against foreign invasions as, for example, did Aḥmad al-Badawī (d. 1276), the "star-gazing" Egyptian saint who defeated the crusade launched by Louis IX. Yet by its very nature Sufism was inward-looking, essentially concentrating on inner development and individual salvation rather than being community-oriented.

Almost by definition, then, Sufism could not encourage, let alone prepare, people for the medical profession and service. Being generally disinclined to formal learning, they were ill-attuned to a profession like medicine. Muslim community matters were hardly of primary importance to them. Further, the essence of the Sufi attitude in general was utter resignation to the will of God and one's inner self-purgation from any extrinsic motivation in worshiping God alone. Even love for God can have a selfish motive (enjoying loving God), and the Sufi sought to raise himself or herself above and beyond fears of punishment and hopes of reward in the hereafter. An early woman Sufi saint, Rābi'a al-'Adawiya (d. 801), addressed God in the following lovely verses:

> I love Thee with two loves, love of my [own] happiness,
> And perfect love, to love Thee as is Thy due.
> My selfish love is that I do naught,
> But think of Thee, excluding all beside;
> But that purest love which is Thy due,
> Is that the veils which hide Thee fall, and I gaze on Thee.
> No praise to me in either this or that,
> Nay, Thine the praise for both that love and this.[10]

The doctrine and practice of this resignation to God is called *tawakkul*, or "trust in God," an essential part of the Sufis' spiritual itinerary, which consists of certain progressive spiritual stations (*maqāmāt*). Often connected with this is the doctrine that one should rise above the "world of causes" (*'ālam al-asbāb*) and rely on God alone. This has been the subject of controversy among the Sufis, for example between two early devout men of the eighth century, Mālik ibn Dinār and Muḥammad ibn Wāsi'. The one held that he would like to own and till a field and thus become independent in his means of livelihood, while the other preferred to have his morning meal without knowing the source of his evening meal.[11] In general, however, the first view prevailed, on the grounds that it would be showing ingratitude to God, and in fact would be going against his will, not to utilize the "world of causes" and to say no to it. Normally, therefore, Sufis got themselves medically treated when they were sick and advocated that their followers do so as well, while relying, perhaps even primarily, on prayer.

·2·

The Religious Valuation of Medicine

The strong element of divine determinism in formal Islamic theology, and the religiopolitical doctrine of Irjā', which in effect meant noninterference in the status quo of the Islamic political, religious, and moral situation, affected to some extent the performance of Muslims in almost all fields of human endeavor. Further, the widespread influence of Sufism in later medieval Islam with its inculcation of the doctrine and attitude of utter resignation to the will of God did militate against human initiative in the arenas of practical life.

This is all true, and yet, as the late H. A. R. Gibb has perceptively remarked, the theological doctrines of Islam had only an oblique or indirect relationship to actual life, and the modern student of theological works in Islam is aptly warned against taking them as being a faithful index to real life. Muslims went about their business in daily life on the assumption that they had to work for their sustenance, that unless they made the necessary endeavor they would get no results (or God would produce no results for them). A Muslim, when sick, knew that he or she had to undertake treatment of the illness, normally physical, but often also spiritual, in order to get well (or, rather, in order for God to cause him or her to get well).

But there is another side to this picture of belief in determinism and resignation to the status quo of things and the Will of God even in theology and religious doctrine itself. Something of the Qur'an's attitude we have seen already. God's vicegerency on the earth means, among other things, that humankind must preserve and develop and beautify God's creation, including human life, and not destroy or spoil it. Of this exercise of divine vicegerency says Muḥammad Iqbāl (d. 1938), addressing God:

You created the night and I created the lamp.
You produced the clay and I fashioned the drinking cup.
You made jungles, meadows, and hills,
And I turned them into flower-beds, lawns, and gardens.[1]

I have already quoted some strong Ḥadīth inducing an attitude of pacifism and compromise or at least accommodation with a morally unwelcome environment. But a good deal of Ḥadīth falls on the other side as well. "Whosoever witnesses evil," says a famous Ḥadīth, "should oppose it with physical strength; if one cannot do this, then one should oppose it with the tongue, and if that cannot be done either, then oppose it with one's heart [or will]—and this last is the weakest form of faith."[2] "A true man of faith is he who speaks out the truth in front of a tyrant," says another well-known tradition.[3] A large number of traditions emphasize social morals. Many of them speak of the obligation to do good to Muslims and guard the interests of the Muslim community, but a good many speak of doing good to all human beings, indeed, to all creatures. There is no doubt that this type of Ḥadīth, together with the heavy emphasis of the Qur'an on socioeconomic justice and egalitarianism, inspired general welfare institutions in Islam. "God has no mercy for the one who has no mercy for the people," said the Prophet, according to most authoritative tradition sources.[4] This type of Ḥadīth seeks to reflect the persistent Qur'anic emphasis on God's limitless mercy and man's niggardliness: "Say (to the Arab pagans, O Muhammad!) 'If you were to possess all the treasures of my Lord's mercy, you would still sit over them out of fear of [becoming poor by] spending them on others'" (17, 100); "Man is by nature unstable; when misfortune touches him, he panics, but when good things come his way, he prevents them from reaching others" (70, 19–21). Without positive works of social weal and alleviation of suffering, prayers [in worship of God] are a mere farce: "Did you see the one who gives the lie to the faith? It is he who maltreats orphans and works little for the feeding of the poor. Woe betide, then, those who pray, yet are neglectful of their prayers" (107, 1–7).

To cite still other traditions: the Prophet said, "People are God's family; the best beloved of God is one who loves his family most." Again, "A person must be devoid of faith if he satiates himself while his neighbor goes hungry." The Prophet said that the Angel of Revelation kept insisting to him so much on good treatment of the neighbor that Muhammad thought the neighbor might become a legal inheritor.[5] "When an orphan cries, God's throne shakes" is another Ḥadīth of this genre.[6] The Prophet's wife 'Āyisha relates that once a Bedouin came to town and held a conversation with the

Prophet, during which he remarked, "You people are in the habit of kissing your children; we do not do this." The Prophet replied, "If God has removed love from your heart, how can I help it?" "A person who helps the widows and the helpless is fighting a Holy War [*jihād*]."[7] Someone asked the Prophet, "How can I know if I am a good man or not?" The Prophet said, "Find out from your neighbors what they think of you."[8] We may end this array of traditions by referring to a popular one about a prostitute who once found a dog gasping out of thirst. She found no water around except a well. She wove her scarf into a sort of rope, tied one of her shoes to it, brought water out of the well, and quenched the dog's thirst. God forgave her sins.[9]

Family ties and especially kind treatment of daughters (which was not generally a strong point in the pre-Islamic Arab character) receives particular attention in the traditions. That one should bring up one's children well is the best service to God one can do, declares one Ḥadīth. The Prophet also said, "A woman who has been widowed, is beautiful, and has a good social position [so that she can easily remarry], but nevertheless devotes herself to her children and brings them up, shall be my companion in heaven and will be close to me like this," and he joined together his middle finger and his index finger. "One's daughter is a wall against hell-fire" is another saying of the Prophet. A person who has a daughter or a sister, is kind to her, brings her up well, and does not give his male children preferential treatment over her is destined for paradise, according to another Ḥadīth. Finally, it is reported that the Prophet said that the best charity a person can give is that, if his daughter is divorced by her husband and she has no economic resources, he supports her.[10] This teaching about the daughter is in conscious contrast to the pre-Islamic Arab practice of female infanticide.

It is true that most of the specific Ḥadīth quoted above about certain acute social and moral problems are probably not the work of the Prophet himself. Nevertheless, they do represent an elaboration of and a commentary upon some key issues treated by the Qur'an and doubtless by the Prophet as well. In other words, they are a genuine extension of the teaching of the Qur'an and the Prophet's example, contrary to the Ḥadīth quoted earlier on Irjā', which also constitute solutions to certain crucial political and religious problems in the early history of the community but which obviously contravene the moral stances of the Qur'an.

So far as positive religious tolerance is concerned, its mainspring in Islam has been Sufism, some of whose asocial aspects we saw above. Sufism was definitely Islamic not just because it was within the Islamic fold and because all great Sufis accepted the religious law of Islam as binding, but also because they did a great deal of missionary work. Nevertheless, their attitude toward the followers of other religions was highly positive. When the great Sufi poet Jalāl al-Dīn al-Rūmī, founder of the Mawlavī (Turkish: Mevlevī) order of dervishes, died in 1273 at Konya (not far from Ankara in Turkey), his funeral service was attended not just by Muslims but by many Greek Orthodox as well. Stories of Sufi ecumenism are so profuse that even if one discounts many of them as apocryphal, there still must remain a core of true ones—quite apart from the fact that even the invention of so many stories by itself tells of their great spirit of positive tolerance. The greatest theosoph among them, the Spanish Ibn al-'Arabī (d. 1240), the grand-master of al-Rūmī, states that one cannot be a true Islamic monotheist unless one subscribes to all religious creeds and that belief in some creeds to the exclusion of others is polytheism.[11] "Moses and the Shepherd," a poem in al-Rūmī's famous and massive Sufi poetic work, the *Mathnavī*, drives this point home. Al-Rūmī tells us that when Moses was going to Mount Sinai to see the Lord,

> Moses saw a shepherd on the way, crying, 'O Lord who choosest as Thou wilt. Where art Thou that I may serve Thee and sew Thy clothes and kill Thy lice and bring milk to Thee, O worshipful one; That I may kiss Thy little hand and rub Thy little feet and sweep Thy little room at bed-time.' On hearing those foolish words, Moses said, 'Man, to whom are you speaking? What babble! What blasphemy and raving! Stuff some cotton into your mouth! Truly the friendship of a fool is enmity, the High God is not in want of such like service!' The shepherd rent his garment, heaved a sigh, and took his way to the wilderness. Then came to Moses a Revelation: 'Thou hast parted my servant from Me. Wert thou sent as a Prophet to unite, or wert thou sent to sever? I have bestowed on everyone a particular mode of worship; I have given everyone a peculiar form of expression. The idiom of Hindustan is excellent for Hindus, the idiom of Sind is excellent for the people of Sind.'[12]

ḤADĪTH AND MEDICINE

In order to assign the contents of this and the following chapter on the Prophetic Medicine to their proper place in history, the reader should give serious consideration to the following observations of Ibn Khaldūn (1332–1406), universally hailed by modern scholarship as a historian who pioneered the sociological approach to the theory of history in his volume titled the *Muqaddima*, or the *Prolegomenon*, to his historical work:

> The Bedouins, in their culture, have a kind of medicine which they base primarily on experience restricted to a few patients only and which they have inherited from their tribal leaders and old women. In some cases it is correct, but it is not founded upon natural laws, nor is it tested against [scientific accounts of] natural constitutions [of people]. Now the Arabs had a great deal of this type of medicine [before Islam] and there were, among them, well-known doctors like al-Ḥārith ibn Kalada and others. The medicine that has been transmitted in Islamic religious works [i.e., in contradistinction to works of scientific medicine] belongs to this genre. It is definitely no part of divine revelation [to Muhammad] but was something customarily practiced among the Arabs. It [this type of medicine] is included in the biographies of the Prophet just as are other matters pertaining to his biographical data that belong to the natural life and customs of the Arabs but form no part of the religion [of Islam] to be practiced in [exactly] that way. For the Prophet had been sent only to teach us the Sacred Law, not medicine or anything else that pertains to customary life—Remember what happened to him with regard to his advice about the fertilization of date-palms, on which occasion he said [to people], "You know better than I matters pertaining to this world." Hence it is improper to regard any medical material that has gone into genuine Ḥadīths transmitted from him as forming part of the Sacred Law, since there is nothing to indicate this. However, if someone uses them [such medicines] by way of seeking God's blessing and with firm faith, they will have palpable effect—except that theirs would not be scientific medicine but would be a result of strong faith, as happened to the one suffering from stomach trouble when treated with honey.[13]

The reference to the fertilization of date-palms is tied to a famous Ḥadīth. Once the Prophet had advised his followers that if they did not resort to artificial fertilization of date-palms, the latter would give better fruit. Later some of them informed him that acting upon his advice they had a bad crop, upon which he said, "About your affairs concerning this world you know better." Noteworthy, too, is Ibn Khaldūn's final sentence in this quotation, which may be understood in two ways. It could be taken as an astute man's safeguard against the reaction of fanatics who might accuse him of disbelief in what he himself has admitted to be "genuine" Ḥadīth from the Prophet, or it may mean, as the last words of the sentence strongly suggest, that resorting to such prescriptions would produce results not scientifically but as cases of faith-healing. The report about honey is based on Qur'an 16, 69, where honey is mentioned as a health-restoring food, and on certain Ḥadīths.[14] Finally, it is quite possible that at least some of the medical Ḥadīth attributed to the Prophet represent his approval of the customary medicine of the Arabs, but there can be little doubt that as time went on, such Ḥadīth multiplied beyond any credible limits.

Medical Ḥadīths from the Prophet, then, can be seen as falling into three categories. The first is the Ḥadīth that encourages medical treatment in case of sickness and seeks to give broad principles of health. The second comprises putative statements of the Prophet on particular diseases and health problems and measures to treat them, whether medically or spiritually. The third is the role of this Ḥadīth in the literature of Prophetic Medicine.

A universally acclaimed statement of the Prophet in Ḥadīth literature is "God has sent down a treatment for every ailment," or "There is a medicine for every ailment such that if a right medicine hits a corresponding ailment, health is restored by God's permission."[15] This Ḥadīth has an important theological point—that medicine does its work *through God's will.* A good deal of such Ḥadīth is advice on eating and drinking and is largely preventive in nature. This seems to have been an important principle in pre-Islamic Arab health care. For example, advice against surfeiting or eating too soon following another meal occurs very often in Ḥadīths. Hygiene also forms an important part. Even ritual ablution before prayer involves regular washing of hands, face, and feet and cleaning teeth before the early morning prayer. Another Ḥadīth states, "A person's body has a due right over him."[16]

"Excessive worry makes for physical illness in a person,"[17] according to a tradition which notes the psychosomatic phenomenon of illness. Although we find examples of treatment of illness through amulets and prayers, it is severely restrained. It is reported that the Prophet had at first forbidden all amulets for fear they contained certain words that compromised the rigorous monotheism of the Qur'an by invoking spirits and other powers. Subsequently, he allowed their use but only if their contents were in accordance with the teaching of the Qur'an and preferably based upon Qur'anic prayers.[18] It is said that he allowed prayer-healing for bites of poisonous animals and for the "evil eye." Belief in the evil eye is very common among the masses in Muslim countries, indeed, in the entire East, and even some well-educated people think it affects adversely the person hit by it. In order to ward off the effects of the evil eye, women particularly say "*mā shā' Allāh*"—"whatever God will," meaning God can create great abilities and beautiful figures, and therefore, for example, a beautiful child or an extraordinarily able person will be protected by God from the evil eye. A person whose evil eye affects another person adversely is supposed to look upon the latter with jealousy: it is the "jealous eye" that so hits.

Omens and star-cults, common in pre-Islamic Arabia, were forbidden. (Star-cult is said to have spread in ancient Arabia as part of pan-Babylonian religion. It was forbidden by the Qur'an itself in 41, 37: "Worship not the sun or the moon but worship God [alone] who created them.") Magic, whether "black" or "white," is forbidden by the Qur'an; its efficacy is accepted but only at the psychological level. The magicians of Pharaoh, who, opposing Moses, threw down their ropes and sticks, "only tricked the eyes of the people" without changing their real character although they even frightened Moses himself (7, 116; 20, 66). Strictly speaking, therefore, all magic is black and evil because it conceals reality as opposed to the "signs" (*āyāt*) or miracles that affect reality. Similarly, its psychological effect is shown in a story of the two fallen angels, Hārūt and Mārūt, who taught people magic in order to "bring about separation between husbands and their wives" (2, 102), that is, through psychological manipulation. As for miracles (supranatural miracles), the Qur'an accepted their actuality at the hands of earlier prophets—from Noah through Jesus—but the Prophet Muhammad himself had none because "they were ineffective even against earlier disbelieving peoples" (17, 59). The peoples of Noah and Abraham, Pharaoh and his people, and the Jews had been impervious to the miracles of Noah, Abraham, Moses, and Jesus respectively. And when, under pressure from his opponents to bring miracles, Muhammad showed signs of anxiety over the fact that miracles were not vouchsafed to him, the Qur'an commented in rather sharp words:

> We know, indeed, that what they say grieves you (O Muhammad!), but the wicked ones are not just rejecting you, they are rejecting the signs of God [the Qur'an]. Messengers before you have been repudiated [by their peoples], but they bore with patience their repudiation and their persecution until our succor came to them. . . . If their rejection [of your message] weighs so heavily upon you, then, if you can, seek out a hole into the earth or [climb up] to the heaven by a ladder and bring them a miracle! If God so wills, he would unite all people on [this] guidance—so do not be among the ignorant ones." (6, 33–35)

Although, therefore, God has the power to create miracles, there shall be henceforth no miracles because they are out-of-date. The Qur'an is, of course, talking of "supranatural" miracles but still upholds other "natural" or "historical" miracles, for example, punishment of evil ones through famine, disease, and so on. The Ḥadīth, nevertheless, recounts a great many of Muhammad's alleged supranatural miracles which must have been concocted by Muslims in rivalry with other communities' accounts of *their* religious founders and leaders. Seen in context, the permission for prayer-healing on the part of Muhammad—for this type of Ḥadīth report does appear to be founded in fact, no doubt with some extrapolations—is seen, then, not as a kind of supranatural miracle but as a natural effect of prayers.

The doctrine of natural miracles was later developed in an elaborate fashion by Ibn Sīnā (d. 1037), the most well known and influential doctor and philosopher in the history of Islam. His argument, however, which starts and develops naturalistically, ends at a point where the lines between natural and supranatural miracles practically vanish (contrary to what we have seen of the Qur'an), although he insists that only "rational miracles are possible" and that the "irrational miracles commonly believed in are absurd."[19] Ibn Sīnā first states that there are physically sick people who get well through sheer willpower, and conversely, there are healthy persons who become obsessed with the idea that they are sick, so that they really become physically sick. From this he concludes that the mind, which belongs to the realm of higher metaphysical principles, "exercises lordship over matter." He illustrates this by saying that if a plank of wood is put across a street and someone is asked to walk on it, he will be able to do so quite easily. But if the same plank of wood is placed across a gorge, the same person will probably not be able to walk on it and may well fall if he tries. The only difference in this case is fear, a mental phenomenon. This again shows that mind exerts a dominating power over the body. Although Ibn Sīnā also holds that the mind is affected by the body—he is an "interactionist" in his view of the mind-body relationship—he nevertheless believes that the mind is the more ultimate and powerful of the two. He concludes that if a mind is exceptionally strong and pure, it can affect not only its own body but others as well. Citing examples of hypnotism or suggestion (*al-wahm al-ʿāmil*) as well as of the "evil eye," he tells us that particularly a person possessing a great, strong, integrated, and holy mind can bring about changes in natural phenomena. This philosophical basis explains cures brought about by suggestion and prayers.

It appears that the Prophet did prescribe certain treatments for sick people. The Ḥadīth is unanimous that the Prophet recommended cupping (blood-letting from certain veins) and the use of honey. For certain stomach ailments he himself used and also prescribed for others a drink made of grain husks, milk, and honey.[20] But, as Ibn Khaldūn says, there is no reason to believe that these medical prescriptions or suggestions were necessarily his own innovations and not part of ancient Arabian medicine. Cupping, for instance, was common in Arabia. But these prescriptions certainly had nothing to do with his religious mission, as many people later took them to be.

There is contradictory Ḥadīth, however, on certain forms of illness and their treatment. For example, there is Ḥadīth that the Prophet had forbidden cauterization, which was common among Arabs for treatment of a morbid condition of flesh. But there is also Ḥadīth that the Prophet ordered it and even performed it himself on persons who had been wounded in war. Nor is the prohibitive Ḥadīth conditional: it says that the Prophet categorically stated, "[although it is restorative of health], I prohibit my community from cautery." Ḥadīth commentators who believe the permission for cauterization to be correct say that the prohibition holds only when cauterization comes to be regarded as a sure, "can't-miss" measure of healing, as many pre-Islamic Arabs regarded it.

As for the etiology of sickness, natural causes of illness are recognized just as natural effects of medication are recognized. Yet the Ḥadīth as well as the Qur'an recognizes several divine purposes of illness. The most frequently mentioned reason for illness, as indeed for other misfortunes, is God's trial of people and the cathartic effect of illness, if it is borne with patience. There is some Ḥadīth according to which the patient even earns merit: the Prophet is reported to have said that if someone has failed to come up to the level of a true person of faith in certain respects, God afflicts him or her with some severe illness or with loss of wealth or bereavement through the death of a dear one, and if patient under these trials, he or she can attain the rank of the truly faithful. There are several Ḥadīths according to which someone who dies of plague or another disease, including a mother who dies in pangs of childbirth, attains the rank of a martyr.[21]

Although in Sunni Ḥadīth, patients are not asked to avoid treatment but encouraged to seek it, in Shiʿa Ḥadīth, patients are strongly advised to bear pain and discomfort of disease and have recourse to a doctor only if disease threatens to become incurable and pain unbearable. According to one Shiʿa Ḥadīth, a person who passes one night in the discomfort of illness earns greater merit than would be gained by worshipping God for one whole year. The Shiʿa tendency to underplay natural cures and to emphasize the value of suffering much more than the Sunnis is undoubtedly connected with the passion motif and the stress on martyrdom, of which Sunni Islam has little trace. A great Shiʿa divine, Muhammad Bāqir al-Majlisi II (d. 1800), is reported to have said, "Sometimes a medicine has no natural relationship with an illness but if it is taken simply on faith—so that a person of strong faith be distinguished from that of weak faith—it will prove beneficial, not because of its natural properties but because of the sincerity and faith of the user." This kind of Ḥadīth is not to be found in Sunni Islam, which also recognizes faith healing, as said before, but only through prayers and amulets. It is because of this attitude that some Shi'a believe that medicine is not based on scientific experiment but rests only on the authority of tradition. Al-Shaikh al-Mufīd, one of the foremost Shi'a theologians and religious authorities (d. 1023), is credited with having said, "[The science of] medicine is correct and its knowledge is attested [to have come] through revelation. Scholars learned this from prophets. For this reason, there is no way to the knowledge of a disease except on the basis of traditional authority, and there is no way to the knowledge of a cure except through divine succor. It is therefore established that the way [to learn medicine] is acquisition through listening to someone who knows hidden things."[22]

It should be pointed out that the belief was very common in medieval Islam that all arts and cultural amenities were first revealed to prophets or discovered through intuition. This is the reverse of Euhemerism, the Greek Enlightenment theory that Greek deities of popular religion were really great men in the distant past who had invented various arts like weaving, agriculture, and medicine and for this reason were deified long after their death. Sunni Islam accepts, like the Shi'a, that the beginnings of human arts and sciences were "revealed" to prophets and that all arts and sciences are in this sense sacred, but they do not generally accept that these must therefore be learned only through traditional authority and not through experimentation and reasoning.

SCIENTIFIC MEDICAL TRADITION AND RELIGIOUS JUSTIFICATION

Works on scientific medicine usually set to their business without explicitly stating the religious value or justification of medicine. They do not, of course, think that medicine is religiously neutral, but they take it for granted. The great and influential Sufi mystic and theologian al-Ghazālī accuses many doctors of his day of publicizing the slogan "First look after your health and then after your religion," whereby, he says, they confuse the priorities of the average man.[23] Al-Ghazālī, of course, does not intend to devalue medicine: he counts medicine among those sciences—like the Sacred Law—which it is not incumbent upon every Muslim man and woman to learn, but what is necessary is that a sufficient number of Muslims learn it to look after the needs of the community, while knowledge of religious duties is incumbent upon every individual Muslim, male and female. The first is called *farḍ al-kifāya*, the second *fard al-'ain*.[24] This is the repeated position of all the representatives of the Prophetic Medicine as well: after faith, the art and practice of medicine is the most meritorious service in

God's sight. In fact, many in the scientific medical tradition itself (for example, Ibn al-Qifṭī, in the introduction to his *Tārīkh al-Ḥukamā'*, or *History of Doctors and Philosophers*, believe that the art of medicine was originally revealed through a prophet, generally named Idrīs (identified with Enoch).

'Alī ibn al-'Abbās al-Majūsī (d. 994), whose comprehensive *The Perfect in the Art* (*Al-Kāmil fī'l-Ṣinā'a*) was the clearest and most commonly consulted medical work before Ibn Sīnā's *Canon* (*Al-Qānūn*), says in the introduction that the basic excellence of humans over animals, for which God be praised, is reason whereby happiness is attained both in this world and in the next—of which medicine is undoubtedly a salient fruit.[25] Al-Sha'rānī, who abridged the large medical work of al-Suwaidī (d. 1292) on "prescriptions established by experience" (*mujarrabāt*), says in his introduction that he has followed the original author in the arrangement of his work; then he adds, "God helps his servant [humankind] so long as the latter serves his brother [other human beings]—so I seek God's help in completing this work."[26] This clearly establishes that medicine is a religious service and that one can hope to receive God's help so long as one helps one's fellow human beings. The early fifteenth-century medical writer al-Azraq tells us in the introduction to *Medical Benefits Made Accessible* (*Tashīl al-Manāfi'*), "Medicine is a science whose benefits are great and whose nobility, prestige, and fame are recognized and *whose roots are established in the Book* [*the Qur'an*] *and the Example* [*sunna*]. . . ."[27] It is clear, then, that both theologians and traditionists who wrote Prophetic Medicine works, on the one hand, and the writers of scientific medicine, on the other, valued medicine as a religious vocation of the first order because it helps men and women to help others preserve and restore their health.

Another reason for the study of medicine is offered in the statement of Abū Bakr Rabī' ibn Aḥmad al-Akhwīnī al-Bukhārī (tenth century C.E.), a well-known disciple of a disciple of the illustrious and perhaps the most scientifically minded medical man of medieval times, Abū Zakarīyā al-Rāzī (Rhazes of the Latin Middle Ages, d. circa 925). In the introduction to his *Guide for Students* (*Hidāyat al-Muta'allimīn*) he says, "Wise men have said that it is incumbent upon every person to learn [the basics] of the Sacred Law, for when a person knows the Sacred Law, he is immune from going astray. Second, he must know some [basic] medicine in order to preserve his health *so that quack doctors will not be able to destroy him.* Third, he must learn some art to earn his livelihood by lawful means."[28] Here are given two reasons for the "vulgarization" of medicine—besides its being counted as being next only to religion in importance—namely, to preserve one's health and to be able to distinguish quacks from sound doctors.

The most illustrious period of Islamic medicine was between the ninth and thirteenth–fourteenth centuries, identified by modern historians of Islamic medicine as "Arabic medicine" because the salient works were almost all written in the Arabic language whether the contributors were Muslims, Christians, Jews, or Zoroastrians or whether they were ethnically Arabs, Persians, Turks, or Jews. In other words, what we are concerned with is a civilization at the heart of which lies Islam as a religion and Arabic as the *lingua franca*. It is true that in the later medieval period, particularly after the advent of the Shiʿa Safavid dynasty in Iran (sixteenth century), many works began to be written in Persian as well.

Under the aegis of modern scholarship, the Islamic-Arab period of medicine has been much studied, although much still remains to be studied. Adolf Fonahn in his *Zur Quellenkunde der Persischen Medizin* (1910) listed 151 works dealing with this period. But, although I do not know them directly, they seem to be concerned with medicine and not the spiritual milieu in which it had its home—the faith of Islam. In 1970, Manfred Ullmann published his *Die Medizin im Islam*, which is an excellent survey of Islamic medicine but which goes frequently wrong when it characterizes the religiocultural milieu wherein this medical tradition grew and developed. The more recent *Vorlesungen über die Medizin im Islam* (1982), by Felix Klein-Franke, is not so much a history of medicine in Islam as a study of its religiocultural milieu.[29] Unfortunately, however, in describing the spiritual impact of Islamic medicine, Klein-Franke is one-sided and passes extreme judgments, whether on orthodox (Ashʿarite) Islam or on the Sufi expression of Islam, so that one wonders how in that environment scientific medicine could exist at all, let alone grow and thrive.

·3·

The Prophetic Medicine

ITS ORIGIN AND CHARACTER

Above, I quoted Ibn Khaldūn to the effect that what the Ḥadīth literature contains of Prophetic Medicine is actually the ancient Bedouin Arab medicine that was based on long experience but not on systematic experimentation, and not, therefore, founded on natural laws. A sound idea of the origin and overall character of this literature requires some analysis of the very early cultural developments in Islam particularly from the perspective of medical history. First, according to an overwhelming number of reports of Muslim historians of medicine, there were, on the eve of Islam and during the Prophet's lifetime, one or two people who knew not just the ancient Arabian medicine but also scientific medicine cultivated at Gundaishāpūr in southwestern Iran, where the Iranian ruler Anūshirwān had invited Greek and Indian medical men to teach at the medical college.[1] These were al-Ḥārith ibn Kalada of the tribe of Banū Thaqīf and his son al-Naḍr ibn al-Ḥārith. Reports are not unanimous about the son's having studied in Iran, but many allege that he studied with his father besides studying the ancient Arabian medicine with others.[2] This background makes highly plausible the reports that the Prophet had advised his companions from time to time to take medicines from al-Ḥārith as he himself had undoubtedly used them. In the following account, we shall refer to several works of the genre of Prophetic Medicine but shall have to rely largely on the work of Abū 'Abd Allāh Muhammad al-Dhahabī, famous traditionist and historian, because he concentrates more on the religious doctrine while others mainly give prescriptions.

Nevertheless, it is equally certain that the large mass of medical traditions contained in Ḥadīth works and later expanded further into thick volumes of Prophetic Medicine (for example, the work of Ibn Qayyim al-Jauzīya, d. 1350, running to nearly four hundred pages) cannot have been the work of the Prophet Muhammad. What can be said, then, about its origin and the causes of its growth within Islam? What led the Muslims to create this genre of literature, running into almost a score of works, alongside the scientific traditions of medicine in Islam? One answer (given, for example, by Ullmann) is that the Islamic orthodoxy wanted thereby to challenge the medical authority of a "pagan Galen" on behalf of the Prophet's authority.[3] A second answer could be that it was an attempt on the part of certain theological authorities to make available to the average educated Muslim a kind of handbook, a "medicine made easy" for the sake of benefiting as many people as possible. For this literature comprises mainly prescriptions for certain defined diseases and has little to do with medical theory beyond commonplace maxims and well-known principles. Third, it may be held that this was an attempt to spiritualize medicine, to set high religious value on it, and to bring it to the center of Islamic concerns. Finally, it may be argued that theologians, who were entrenched opponents of philosophy and its typical representatives like Ibn Sīnā, the philosophical bête noire of the orthodoxy but also the most famous medical name in the Middle Ages, were anxious to wrest medicine from them and "Islamize" it by making it independent of philosophy and its presuppositions.

Although the first three explanations have some validity, the aim of spiritualizing medicine gave, I believe, the greatest impetus. The first, challenging the "pagan Galen" in the Prophet's name, is probably the weakest and occurs at a very late stage in the development of this literature. Against this explanation, it may be urged that authors of Prophetic Medicine works mainly combine traditional medicines and maxims with principles of Greek medicine. Ibn al-Jauzi (d. 1200) states in the introduction to his eclectic work *Beneficial Selections from Medicine* that he has taken into consideration the traditions from the Prophet and his companions just as much as he has included the doctrines of the men of medical science. Al-Dhahabī (d. 1348) also says in the introductory remarks to his *Prophetic Medicine*, "I sought guidance from God [the term used in several such works is *istikhāra*, a technical religious term which means that before undertaking a work of special importance one performs ablutions, offers prayer to God, and then rests, relaxes, or sleeps so that the right decision is cast in his mind by God] concerning making a collection of certain medical traditions of the Prophet and the traditions of medical doctors such as are necessary for preserving health when it exists or restoring it when it is not there."[4] Two authors in the fourteenth century (Ibn Qayyim al-Jauzīya, d. 1350, and al-Surramarrī, d. 1374) clearly state that the relationship between the divinely revealed medicine and that of the medical doctors (Galen, Ibn Sīnā, and so on) is like the relationship between this latter medicine and superstitions of folk medicine.[5] Nevertheless, both of them quote Arab medical authorities and Christian, Jewish, and Muslim doctors as well.

What, then, does this dictum mean and what does it mean to say that the Prophetic Medicine is "divinely revealed"? Ibn Qayyim tells us that Prophetic Medicine deals with the overall principles while scientific medicine fills in the details. What this assertion means is perhaps to be found in Ibn Qayyim's statements about the nature of man as not being merely a body alone but also a mental-spiritual entity. After mentioning the various methodologies of the medical tradition—reasoning by deductive analogy (*qiyās*), experimentation and observation done on animals (*tajriba, mushāhada*), and "right intuition"—he says:

> Where do these stand in relation to revelation that God sends to his Messenger about what is beneficial to him and what is harmful? The relationship of their medicine to the revelation is like the relationship of their science and learning to the teaching that the prophets have brought. There are, indeed, therapies whither the intellects of even the great doctors have not repaired, and where their sciences, experiments, and deductive analogies have not led them. For example, spiritual therapies and the strength of the heart that comes [only] from faith in God and trust in him, charity and prayer, repentance and seeking God's forgiveness, doing good to mankind, helping the helpless and relief of the afflicted. For these medicines have been [successfully] tried by communities, with all their differences in religions and faiths, and have been found by them to have healthful effects which cannot be attained [only] by science, experiments, and the deductive analysis of medical men. We and others like us have tried these matters often and found them to have an efficacy not possessed by material medicines—indeed, these medicines in relation to them are just like soothsayers' medicine in relation to scientific medicine. And all this is in accordance with the law of God's wisdom [operative in nature], nothing outside it. But the causes according to which this law operates are varied. When man's heart becomes attuned to the Lord of the world, the creator of ailments and remedies, who governs nature according to his will, other medicines become available that cannot be experienced by an unbelieving and indifferent heart. It has been experienced that when man's spirit becomes strong and also the soul and bodily nature are strengthened, they cooperate in repelling disease and overcoming it, and this cannot be denied except by the most ignorant of people.[6]

This argument does not deny the efficacy of physical cures but rather points to the integrity of the human person. This explains why the medicines of Galen and Ibn Sīnā were considered inferior to the Prophet's medicine. The same threefold distinction between the spirit, soul, and physical nature made in the above passage appears in the work of his contemporary al-Dhahabī but without casting any slur on Galen. For al-Dhahabī, the benefits of Islamic ritual prayers, which involve certain changing physical postures, are fourfold—spiritual, psychological, physical, and moral:

> Prayers can cause recovery from the pain of the heart, stomach, and intestines. There are three reasons for this. First, it is a divinely commanded form of worship. Second, it has a psychological benefit. This is because prayers divert the mind from the pain and reduce its feeling whereby the power to repel [the cause of] pain is strengthened. Expert doctors try all means to strengthen this [natural] power—sometimes by feeding something, sometimes by inspiring hope, and sometimes by inspiring fear. Now, prayer [with concentration] combines most of these means of benefit, because it at once instills fear, self-effacing humility, love [of God], and remembrance of the Last Day. . . . It is related about one of ʿAlī's children that he needed some surgery, but the doctors could not perform it [for fear of causing pain]. His family then left him alone until he embarked upon prayers, when they were able to do the surgery —he did not shrink or shrivel because he was deeply concentrating upon prayers. Abū Ayyūb [al-Anṣārī] used to order his children to keep quiet at home. But he allowed them to talk when he entered upon his prayers; he said to them, "When I am in prayer, I do not hear your voice." Once a wall collapsed while he was in prayer, but he was not perturbed.
>
> Third, in prayer, there is a physical factor as well, besides the concentration of the mind, namely, the exercise of the body. This latter is due to the fact that prayers contain the postures of standing upright, genuflexion, prostration, relaxation, and concentration; where bodily movements occur and most bodily organs relax. Al-Muwaffaq ʿAbd al-Laṭīf narrates in his *Kitāb al-Arbaʿīn* [a book comprising forty Ḥadīths concerning health and medicine—such books were written by many people], "I have seen a number of people who led lazy lives because of their wealth, who nevertheless had preserved good health. When I investigated the cause of this, I found that they were given to frequent prayer and also to regular *tahajjud* [midnight prayer]."[7]

After detailing the physical benefits of the various postures, al-Dhahabī continues:

> "Prayers often produce happiness and contentment in the mind; they suppress anxiety and extinguish the fire of anger. They increase love for truth and humility before people; they soften the heart, create love and forgiveness and dislike for the vice of vengeance. Besides, often sound judgment occurs to the mind [due to concentration about difficult matters] and one finds correct answers [to problems]. One also remembers forgotten things. . . . One can discover the ways to solve matters worldly and spiritual. And one can effectively examine oneself—particularly when

> one strenuously exercises oneself in prayers. The best time is [past] midnight when people are asleep and there is no noise."[8]

This integrality of the health of the whole person—spiritual, psychological, physical, and moral—is the essence of the message of the so-called Prophetic Medicine.

A second motivation behind the Prophetic Medicine was to give the general educated public easy access to preventive and curative measures. One writer of these works after another declares that he undertook his work in order to enlarge the benefit of medicine for as many people as possible. This explains why there is little or no theory in them; they are filled with medical advice and prescriptions—physical and spiritual and occasionally magical cures as well. The title of such a work as Ibn al-Jauzi's *Beneficial Selections from Medicine* indicates both the eclectic composition of the work and its popular nature. Another early fifteenth-century writer, Ibrāhīm ibn 'Abd al-Raḥmān al-Azraq, titled his work *Medical Benefits Made Accessible.* In the introduction he writes, "When I saw that [today] there are very few people who concern themselves with medicine but those who seek help from it are many, and this art being buried under the great and common need for it on the part of people, it appeared to deserve special devotion since no human being can avoid it. Al-Aḥnaf ibn Qais said, 'No intelligent man can afford to abandon three types of knowledge—the knowledge of that which he can take as his provision for the next life, the knowledge whereby he can establish his worldly life which [in turn] will help him in establishing his faith, and thirdly, such knowledge of medicine as can help repair his ailments.' This, then, motivated me to collect [compile] certain materials concerning this art."[9] This popularizing of medicine was done, therefore, as an act of piety. Obviously there was no commercial enterprise involved in it, nor were the authors even in a single case financially subsidized by a patron, as was the case with many scientist-doctors who received the patronage of some prince, ruler, or other rich benefactor. Nor, finally, did such authors normally practice medicine, for they were primarily theologians and religious leaders. If any did so, they did it as a pious hobby "to earn the reward in the hereafter."

This brings us directly to the third of the motivations of the Prophetic Medicine literature, to bestow high religious value upon it and, in fact, to bring it to the center of the faith. In the introduction to his *Prophetic Medicine* al-Dhahabī writes,

> It is incumbent upon every Muslim to seek nearness to God in every possible way that can bring him near unto God and to do his utmost in obe-

> diently carrying out God's commands. Now, the most beneficial of such means and the most consequential of approaches to God—after obeying his direct commandments and desisting from his explicit prohibitions—is that which benefits humanity in terms of preserving their health and treating their ailments, since health is among those things which have been required in the prayer forms of worship laid down in the Sacred Law.[10]

Along with others, the same author quotes al-Shāfi'ī (d. 819), founder of the Shāfi'ī school of law (one of the four Sunni schools of law), as having said, "I do not know of any type of knowledge, after the knowledge of what is lawful and what is unlawful, more noble for a Muslim [to acquire] than that of medicine but, alas! they have neglected it—they have neglected one-third of human knowledge—and abandoned it to Jews and Christians!"[11] In the context of the religious valuation of medicine, a Ḥadīth attributed to the Prophet is also quoted: "[Valid or beneficial] knowledge is only of two kinds, knowledge of faith and knowledge of the body."[12]

Ḥadīths have already been cited to the effect that illness and pain had the triple function of trial from God, of expiation of sins, and of reward in the future, particularly in the afterlife, provided one bears the affliction with steadfastness. Works on the Prophetic Medicine add new points, for example, that illness often leads a person to repent of sins and therefore has a reformative and redemptive effect on his or her character. Whereas the works of Ḥadīth proper say that the Prophet declared death from certain diseases like the plague or stomach trouble (*al-mabṭūn*) to be equivalent to martyrdom, the Prophetic Medicine generalizes and says that according to the Prophetic statement "Whoever dies in any illness is a martyr." According to yet another Ḥadīth the Prophet said, "I find strange on the part of a man of faith that he should grieve at his ailment; if he knew what [goodness] is in his illness, he would love to be ill until he meets His Lord."[13] It should be remembered in this connection that in pre-Islamic Arabia, natural death or "death on bed" for men was considered much inferior to death in fighting and was sometimes referred to almost as a term of contempt. An even more spectacular statement has been attributed to the Prophet: "Most of the martyrs of my community are those who died bedridden; as for many of those who die in the battlefield fighting for Islam [in *jihād*, or the holy war], God knows what their real motivation was," that is, whether they were really fighting for the cause of God or for worldly victory and material success, in which latter case their death in the battlefield is anything but martyrdom.

On the other hand, we find Ḥadīth in this literature that state exactly the reverse, extolling health as the greatest blessing of God after faith and, in fact, as strengthening faith. Says al-Dhahabī in his *Prophetic Medicine*, "Health is the most excellent of God's blessings upon man after [the faith] Islam, for without it man can neither carry on his life business well nor can he obey God's commands. There is, in fact, no other good like it, so man must be thankful for it and not ungrateful, for God's Messenger—peace and blessings of God be upon him—said, 'There are two blessings for which so many people are enviable, health and lack of worry.'" Further, the Prophet said, "There are some of God's servants [that is, human beings] whom God carefully saves from being killed and from illness; he causes them to live in health and to die in health and bestows upon them the honor of martyrs."[14] Death in illness, then, was martyrdom, and now death in good health was regarded as equivalent to martyrdom. Both types of Ḥadīth are quoted by al-Dhahabī in different sections of the same work. We must first conclude that nothing of this has to do with the Prophet at all, but both kinds of Ḥadīth are the work of later Muslims themselves. Yet, despite their being contradictory at face value, each has its own meaning and role in a different context: healthy people, who are able to carry on their own business rather than burdening others—in fact, helping those who are in need—and then even die without others having to expend time, energy, and money, are people who have given to life more than they have taken out of it; they surely deserve the status and reward akin to that of a martyr. But how about a person who is ill, who has not deliberately brought on his illness, bears his illness and pain with patience, tries treatments created by God and discovered by humans, provides others the opportunity to give of their mercy—is he or she any less than a martyr?

These examples, in fact, display the unique value of Ḥadīth, for, despite the fact that its attribution to the Prophet, at least for the most part, may be historically unsound, it is a highly synthetic product, representing a whole spectrum of points of view on a given subject. Indeed, in its spirit it represents a massive commentary by early generations of Muslims on the Qur'an and the Prophet's activity, and even those Ḥadīths that appear to violate both the letter and the spirit of the Qur'an have a valid role when interpreted *in their historical context*. They have proved damaging to Islamic spirituality only because they were seen and blindly believed in by later Muslims without any reference to their originally intended role and their context, which only historical criticism can provide.

We shall consider a few more statements on health and its spiritual value. A companion of the Prophet, Abu'l-Dardā', said to the Prophet, "I much prefer to be in good health and be grateful for it than be afflicted with ill health and bear it with patience," upon which the Prophet replied, "God prefers you to be in good health." This Ḥadīth decides between the two conditions, health with goodness and illness with patience, and finds in favor of the former. In this connection, certain non-Prophetic sayings are also given by the same author: "Health is the crown on the heads of the healthy which is perceived only by those who are sick," and "Health is a blessing of which little awareness is shown by people [who are healthy]." Finally, the Prophet said, "Ask of God His forgiveness and health: for, after faith, no one can get a greater good than health."[15]

Because of this contradiction or (if they are considered in their proper contexts and their goals) tension within Ḥadīth, Muslim scholars came to hold different opinions on whether it is religiously obligatory or only permissible to treat illness. For the Qur'an, because health is God's blessing and its opposite is his wrath or trial—recall Abraham's statement, for example, "When *I* fall sick, *God* restores me to health" (26, 80)—one must pursue it as a religious obligation. But, as has become abundantly clear by now, Ḥadīth and theological opinion go far beyond the Qur'an in interpreting it. Al-Dhahabī, while discussing these opinions, says that all Muslims are agreed that it is good and meritorious to get medically treated when one is sick because of the categorical command of the Prophet, "Get medical treatment."[16]

It is equally religiously obligatory to preserve health when one is not sick because the Prophet did this. He did not overeat, and he prepared his food carefully. We are told that since the Prophet was often taken ill in the last years of his life (particularly after Arab tribes became Muslim and he was frequently visited by their delegations to get instruction in Islam), he was also often seen by doctors and treated.[18] His youngest and most beloved wife 'Āyisha, when asked by people how she came to be knowledgeable about medicine, replied that she got this experience precisely because of the Prophet's frequent illnesses and their treatment.[19]

There are, on the other hand, several traditions (not attributed to the Prophet) according to which it is better not to be medically treated than to be treated, although these are not as uncompromising as the Shi'a Ḥadīth quoted above. The majority of these are attributed to the extreme right-wing traditionist-jurist of the ninth century Aḥmad ibn Ḥanbal (d. 855), who is reported to have said, "Medical treatment is permissible, but its abandonment is better." But it is also reported from him, in another tradition, that treatment is religiously obligatory.[20] These traditions are essentially based on the idea of *tawakkul* (trust in God or resignation to the will of God). In this extreme form, it is patently a Sufi idea, and it is likely that these traditions emanate from the early phase of Sufism which was characterized by asceticism. Felix Klein-Franke narrates a story about an early Sufi woman-saint, Rābi'a al-'Adawiya, whose poetry on divine love was quoted above. According to this story, 'Abd al-Raḥmān ibn 'Āmir says:

> I and Sufyān al-Thawrī visited Rābi'a [once] when she was sick. I could not bring myself to speak to her out of a sense of respect. I said to Sufyān, "Say something." He said [to her], "If you pray to God, he will ease your suffering." She turned her face toward him and said, "O Sufyān! do you not know who has willed my suffering? Is it not God?" He replied, "Yes." She said, "If you know this, why do you ask me to pray for what contradicts his will?"

Thus she opposes not only medical treatment but also prayer for relief, an attitude in keeping with the spirit of divine love. Klein-Franke generalizes that this story "clarifies the attitude of the God-fearing in Islam."[21] But most Sufis, besides praying, got medical treatment when they were ill and also advocated it to their followers. It is therefore not legitimate to make from the practice of some Sufis of the ascetic type, generalizations for all Sufis.

Al-Dhahabī, after giving both sides of this controversy, formulates his answer, which is not only the correct orthodox answer but also that of Sufism: "*Tawakkul* is to trust God by one's own heart. But this does not contradict natural causes nor their use. Indeed, *tawakkul* itself presupposes acceptance of causation—for an expert doctor first tries his best by way of treatment *and then puts his trust in God for his success.* Similarly a farmer tills the soil and sows the seed and [only] then trusts in God that the crop would grow . . . God the exalted has said, 'Take your guard [against peril]' " (Qur'an 4, 71, 102).[22] Several Ḥadīths from the Prophet do extol the spiritual merit of illness and its expiatory function and hold up death in illness as a sort of martyrdom. But these do not say that one should therefore eschew treatment, nor are they in their spirit incompatible with the ideology of treatment.

RELIGION AND MEDICINE-AS-AN-INEXACT-SCIENCE

The preceding discussion brings us face to face with the real problem that underlies all controversies in Islam about the spiritual value of medicine, that is, the issue whether it is more meritorious for the sick to get medical treatment or, rather, to have "trust in God's power and mercy."

We have seen that the vast majority holds that medical treatment has spiritual value and religious merit, that it is even religiously obligatory. There has, however, always been a small minority holding the view that medicines are not religiously *required* and a still more tiny minority holding that it is religiously even more meritorious *not* to have medical treatment but have simple "trust in God." In many a tradition attributed to the Prophet he is asked by someone whether he or she should get treatment, that is, whether natural medicine has religious sanction and natural efficacy, and the Prophet replies in the affirmative. In one tradition, he is asked how medicines can work *against* the decree of God, and he replies, "Medicines are part of the decree of God."[23] According to some historical accounts, 'Umar I, the second caliph of Islam, who was visiting Syria in 638, retreated when he heard that plague had broken out in al-Jābiya, and he also ordered the immediate evacuation of the Muslim army from that place. The Muslim commander of the local forces, an early companion of the Prophet, Abū 'Ubaida ibn al-Jarrāḥ, said to him, "Are you fleeing from God's decree?" to which 'Umar is said to have replied, "Yes, I am fleeing from God's decree into God's decree," meaning that God had decreed the breakout of pestilence in that particular area but had decreed safety in other areas whither he must repair with Muslim forces in order to be safe.[24]

The point to be established is that the worry of those who would rather "rely on God's decree" than on natural measures—apart from whatever other questions they may have in mind of the omnipotence, omniscience, and all-comprehensive wisdom and providence of God—is basically connected with the lack of certainty of medical cures producing expected results. It is the issue of the surety of the outcome that is at stake: God's will is certain to come off, but how certain are medical measures?

This issue is brought effectively home by a related controversy: Can a Muslim use as medicine things that the religious law has prohibited, for example, alcohol or pig's flesh or fat? On the eating of the pig, wherever the Qur'an (2, 173; 6, 145; 16, 115) mentions a prohibition, it always makes an exception for "cases where it may be necessary, without willful transgression of the Law." On alcohol, which the Qur'an severely denounces without giving an outright and explicit prohibition (5, 90–91), all schools of Islamic law prohibit it except the Ḥanafi school, which holds in theory that it is actual intoxication and not consumption of alcohol as such (except that which is extracted from grapes) that is prohibited. Many jurists who totally prohibit the consumption of alcohol allow its use for medicinal purposes. But many do not. We are told that Ibn Ḥanbal and several others do not allow medicines prepared by non-Muslims for fear they may have used ingredients whose consumption is not allowed to Muslims.[25]

The famous jurist-theologian Ibn Taimīya (d. 1328), the teacher of Ibn Qayyim al-Jauzīya, was asked about the use of items that are unlawful for a Muslim to consume, as medicine or as an ingredient in medicine, if they are prescribed as necessary by a doctor. Ibn Taimīya replied that their use is unlawful for medicinal purposes even though their consumption is allowed as food if nothing else is available and death seems imminent because of hunger or thirst. Under such conditions, one can and even must eat pig or drink alcohol. Ibn Taimīya's argument is that if one is hungry and eats swine's flesh, he is certain to be satiated, for that is what food, lawful or unlawful, does. But if one eats it as medicine, the result is not certain, for the efficacy of medicine is never as certain as the efficacy of food is. That which is unlawful in religion cannot be made lawful on the basis of something merely conjectural. Many people regain their health without treatment, so that treatment is not even medically necessary. Ibn Taimīya is one of those theologians who do not consider treatment of the sick as *religiously* necessary but only permissible on the grounds of the uncertainty of its *medical* efficacy: not only do people get well without medicine, but often they do not get well with medical treatment either.[26] This, then, is the basic reasoning of some theologians in Islam who do not set a high value on the medical art (although, as I have demonstrated, most, indeed, do).

Finally, some mention should be made of the salient features of the Prophetic Medicine literature. Perhaps the most important is the great predilection it shows for simple medicines (*al-adwiya al-mufrada* or *al-basīṭa*) as opposed to compound (*al-murakkaba*) medicines. Klein-Franke holds that this is because of the possibility that these latter would contain ingredients forbidden by Islamic law to Muslims. (Al-Dhahabī's view, given above, concerns only those medicines that are prepared by non-Muslims.) One real reason appears to be that compound medicines are likely to have more side effects. This however does not wholly explain the general theological aversion to compounds. Ibn Qayyim al-Jauzīya clarifies this point:

> It belongs to the Prophet's guidance that he got himself medically treated and he commanded other sick persons to do so from among his family and his followers. But it does not belong to his guidance nor to that of his companions to use these compound medicines known as *aqrābādhīn* [a common name for compound medicines in Muslim medicine, an equivalent of *al-adwiya al-murakkaba*]. Most of their medicines were simple, although sometimes was added to these something that would increase their effectiveness or moderate their excess. This, in fact, is by and large the medicine of different peoples with their ethnic diversity—Arabs, Turks, and all desert dwellers. Compound medicines have been the concern mostly of Greeks and Byzantines, while most Indian medicines consist of

> simple ones. All doctors are agreed that if treatment is possible through diet, medicines should not be resorted to, and whenever restoration of health is possible through simple medicines, compound ones should be avoided. They say that whenever illness can be repelled by food to be given and food to be avoided [positive and protective food prescriptions], medicines should not be used. The basis of this is that medicines belong to the same genre as foods. Those people whose foods are for the most part simple have very few ailments, and their treatment also consists of simple medicines. But city dwellers who are used to compound foods need compound medicines as well.[27]

It is to be noted that the last part of this passage concerning the contrast between city dwellers and desert dwellers has strong similarity with the view of Ibn Khaldūn, but there is a contrast in the intent. Whereas Ibn Qayyim al-Jauzīya is praising Bedouin medicine (and it is true that they are incomparably healthful), Ibn Khaldūn, whose purpose in his *Prolegomenon* is to study the development of culture (*al-'Umrān*) and its complexities, regards the Bedouin medicine as primitive, like Bedouin life, even though he praises their health and prowess and their "nearness to nature."[28] In the scientific medical tradition in Islam, pharmacology (dealing with simple medicines) and pharmacy (dealing with compound medicines) are sharply distinguished and practically always treated in separate works, but they receive about equal treatment. In the Prophetic Medicine tradition pharmacology is far more prominent than pharmacy. In the Greek tradition, too, the term *graphidion* applied to synthetic medicines or pharmacy means "the small treatise" (the Arabic *aqrābādhīn* comes from the Greek through Syriac mediation). But in Islam pharmacology, or the science of *materia medica*, became far more highly developed than it was among the Greeks and until recently was regarded by Western historians of medicine as the main contribution of Islam to medicine. The development of pharmacology in Islam probably owes much to the great religious emphasis placed upon it by the representatives of the Prophetic Medicine.

Second, again under religious impulse, the Prophetic Medicine looks with great disfavor upon the use of such ingredients in medicine as may cause harm or even death when taken singly, for example, poisons. Similarly, a compound known as *tiryāq* (an antidote for snakebite) was prohibited in this literature because it contained flesh of snakes and alcohol.[29] So was the milk of she-asses—in fact, all consumables which the religious law has forbidden but which some Muslim medical doctors used as medicine are prohibited by the Prophetic Medicine.[30]

Third, preventive medicine (*al-ḥimya*), although it is an important principle also in the scientific tradition of Islamic medicine, receives special emphasis in the Prophetic Medicine literature. The Qur'anic verse "Eat, drink, but do not commit excesses [in eating and drinking]" (7, 31) is quoted by almost all writers of this genre of literature and is regarded as the ultimate basis of prevention of sickness. Prevention, in this context, means two things: first, taking measures in diet and general hygiene so that one remains free from disease, and second, taking such measures during illness that, when illness is temporarily in abeyance, give the body strength to repel sickness completely. Salmā, daughter of Qais the Anṣārī (that is, belonging to Anṣār, the Medinese population of the Prophet's days who gave refuge to the Prophet when he emigrated from Mecca in 622 and helped him establish Islam both as religion and state), relates,

> Once, the Prophet came to us accompanied by 'Alī [his cousin and son-in-law]. 'Alī was recovering from illness and was physically weak at the time. We had some preripe dates hanging from trees. The Prophet stood up and began eating. 'Alī also started eating. The Prophet said to him, "Take it easy, O 'Alī! You're quite weak [and therefore may not be able to digest them]." 'Alī sat down and did not eat, while the Prophet ate. Then I made a compound of honey and barley. The Prophet said to 'Alī, "By all means, partake of this, for this will agree with your health."

The Prophet is reported once to have reproached a person for eating ripe dates while he was suffering from an eye trouble which is aggravated by sweet ripe dates.[31] Al-Ḥārith ibn Kalada, graduate of the medical school of Gundaishāpūr, in reply to a question as to what was the essence of medicine," said, "prevention"; this story is common in Muslim histories of medicine.[32]

DIETARY LAWS

The Qur'an forbids the eating of swine and the consumption of "blood which has been shed." Criticizing the Arab pagan taboos on eating certain animals (6, 139ff.), the Qur'an says, "Say (O Muhammad!), I do not find in the revelation vouchsafed to me any food unlawful that one might eat except a corpse, or blood that has been shed [of an animal] or the flesh of a swine—for it is unclean—or an unrighteous food, namely, that which has been consecrated to another's name than God's. But whosoever is constrained to eat these without rebelling or transgressing [against God's law], your Lord is forgiving and merciful" (6, 146). In 6, 147 other Jewish taboos are rejected. While the Qur'an apparently prohibited the blood "that has been shed," Muslims have generally come to believe that a slaughtered animal must be cleared of all blood, and they insist that adequate blood-letting can be ensured only by cutting the jugular vein of an animal. Many Muslims, therefore, do not eat meat produced by modern Western butcher-houses; while a few of them eat kosher meat, many others arrange to slaughter their own animals in the traditional Islamic way. The second problem connected with meat is that the Qur'an (6, 122) had prohibited the eating of meat of an animal upon whom "God's name has not been recited." The Ḥanafī school, taking these words at their face value, prohibits all meat upon which the name of God has not been recited. The Shāfi'ī school, however, followed by the Ḥanbalī and Mālikī schools (the Shi'a hold the position similar to the Ḥanafīs), holds that this prohibition cannot be accepted at face value. They argue that basically what has been prohibited is the meat of an animal that has been offered to any other being except God, as has been shown by the Qur'anic quotation. They say that when certain butchers in Mecca became Muslim, they were suspected by Muslims of mentioning their erstwhile gods' names "in their hearts" while slaughtering animals. Muslims therefore stopped buying meat from them. The Qur'anic command to recite God's name while slaughtering animals was explained, then, as being conditional upon a situation where meat-slaughterers might associate the name of someone else with God. But in a situation where there was no such suspicion it was not thought necessary to recite God's name. The adoption of this liberal interpretation enables many Muslims to buy meat prepared by non-Muslim butchers in the West.

It has been noted that alcohol was prohibited by the Qur'an. It is clear from the development of this theme in the Qur'an that its ban on alcohol was reluctant and finally precipitated by feuding among some of the Prophet's followers while they were intoxicated (5, 90–91). For this reason, the Ḥanafī school adopted a liberal attitude toward alcohol and essentially regarded only intoxication by, and not consumption of, alcohol as proscribed. Other schools of law, however, kept pressure on them so that although the Ḥanafīs in theory continued to be liberal, in practice they have fallen in line with the view of the other schools (they still allow it for medical purposes, however). Drugs are also forbidden by the majority of jurists although some, particularly the Shi'a, have assumed a lenient attitude because drugs are not explicitly mentioned in the Qur'an. However, this omission is due to the fact that drug addiction was practically unknown in Arabia, whereas consumption of alcohol was widespread.

MEDICAL ATTITUDES TOWARD CERTAIN ORTHODOX RESTRICTIONS

The Prophetic Medicine literature is a product of theologians and religious personalities who are often extremely puritanical and carry their piety to excess. It is therefore all the more striking that they should have appropriated medicine and indeed brought it to the center of religious doctrine and practice—most of them allowing for medicinal purposes things prohibited by the Sharī'a law. In addition, their literature surprisingly dispenses with sex segregation and the prohibition of music, restrictions which have come to be closely identified with fundamental Islam.

In fact, the Qur'an had not imposed such sex segregation as developed later in Islam: it advises simply that in mixed gatherings, men and women should exercise "sex-modesty" (24, 30–31). This admonition presupposes that there was no sex segregation of the kind called *purdah* which later settled on Muslim societies. Within that code of behavior, not only were the sexes totally segregated but women were required to veil themselves when they went out of their home and, indeed, even from their male relatives. Although no particular date can be assigned to the introduction of sex segregation, it seems to have begun in the eighth century C.E. through influences from Iran after the conquest of that country and mingling of the populations in Iraq, but it was first restricted to the upper classes. Al-Dhahabī, a student of that great orthodox personage Ibn Taimīya, whose views on the prohibition of the medicinal use of things unlawful in the Sharī'a law were noted above, writes in the *Prophetic Medicine* (unfortunately, most works of this genre still remain unpublished and many are probably irretrievably lost[33]), that in cases of illness, if it becomes necessary, it is legitimate for women to treat men and vice versa and for them to look at and examine each other's sexual organs.[34] It is known that before Islam, Arab women used to accompany their fighters to the battlefield where they recited poetry to incite men to fight bravely and treated the wounded and the sick. This practice continued in Islam and indeed was encouraged by the Prophet. The Medinese woman Umm 'Aṭiya, a nurse and companion of the Prophet, reports, "I accompanied the Prophet in seven battles. I rode behind men in their saddles; I used to prepare food for them, treat the wounded and the sick." Anas ibn Mālik, another companion, reports, "The Prophet, on his military campaigns, was accompanied by Umm Sulaim [Anas's mother]; with her were other women from the Anṣār [Medinese Muslims] who provided water [to the soldiers] and treated the wounded."[35] Ahmad ibn Ḥanbal, generally considered to be the most orthodox of all founders of Islamic law, reportedly held the view that it is permissible for a doctor to examine a woman, and if necessary also her sexual organs, and similarly a woman may do the same to a man. Al-Marwazi relates that once Abū 'Abd Allāh was stricken with *lawā* (pain in the stomach due to intestinal convulsions or lumbago in the back, which were treated by massage); he called in a woman, who treated him by massage.[36] There are also other traditions to the same effect.

From the earliest times, Islamic orthodoxy had banned music (apparently on the grounds that it can overly relax the ego and also could become an addiction) as it had prohibited representative arts. It is doubtful if the ban dates from the time of the Prophet himself; but it probably arose a generation or so after him. So far as the Prophetic Medicine literature is concerned, some authors are in favor of the ban, others allow it for women and prohibit it for men, and still others allow it in general. One main consequence of the ban on music was the rise and development of the highly refined and sophisticated art of Qur'an recital (*tajwīd*), cultivated all over the Muslim world and practiced so frequently in various social contexts and religious rituals (the number of those who have memorized the entire Qur'an by heart in the world of Islam must exceed one million even at a conservative estimate). Despite this ban, however, music was widely patronized by princely courts all through the Middle Ages. It was also used in hospitals. From about the ninth or tenth century, Sufis started the practice of *samā'* (spiritual concerts) in order to induce mystical ecstasy,[37] and although the orthodox 'Ulama opposed it in the beginning, their opposition slowly gave way before Sufi persistence. The great thirteenth-century Sufi poet al-Rūmī refers in his *Mathnavī* to his musical instrument:

> Its head, its veins (strings), and its skin are
> all desiccated and dead.
> Whence comes, then, the Voice of my Friend?[38]

That is to say, it is not the instrument itself that speaks but God who speaks through it.

Although in the Qur'an nothing is directly said about music one way or the other, one may guess that it looks upon melodious voice with favor from its statement "The most repulsive voice is the voice of donkeys" (31, 19). By the time of al-Dhahabī, good singing had come to be looked upon as soul-lifting (in fact, in later Islamic tradition, particularly in belles-lettres, David's singing had become proverbial). Says al-Dhahabī, "Singing is the soul's pleasure, the heart's delight and food for the spirit; it constitutes part of the most exalted spiritual medicine. It is pleasurable even to some animals. Its moderate enjoyment kindles natural warmth, strengthens the activity of the various faculties, slows down aging, and repels many diseases." Abū Nu'aim (d. 1038), the theologian and man of piety who was among the first to write a work on the Prophetic Medicine, reports from the Prophet that "music beautifies and refreshes the body just as excessive worry ails it." The best part of singing is, of course, the melodious recital of the Qur'an because, apart from the beauty of its words, the soul benefits from its lofty ideas. The Prophet said, "embellish the Qur'an with your beautiful voices." For reasons that are not quite clear, al-Dhahabī takes the Qur'anic words "God augments his creation by whatever he wills" as referring to music—perhaps because music expands the soul and gives impetus to man's creative activity.[39] In the Islamic philosophical tradition, it was believed (for example, by Mullā Ṣadrā, d. 1641) that Pythagoras had spiritually ascended to the heavens and composed music after the pattern of the sweet melodies he had heard there.[40] The great Egyptian Sufi Dhu'l-Nūn (d. 860), when asked about music, allegedly replied, "It invades [the soul] from God and drives the heart to the good." Al-Dhahabī says that music is bad when it prevents a person from attending to his duties, particularly God's worship, but otherwise it is lawful and good; David had a lovely voice. The Prophet is reported to have said about his companion Abū Mūsa al-Ash'arī, "This person has been given [by God] one of the musical instruments of David." Al-Dhahabī also points out that people whose profession entails hard work make up songs for themselves and sing them to lessen the drudgery of their labor.[41]

After quoting Ibn Qutaiba (d. 889), a famous ninth-century man of letters, a profound defender of Ḥadīth, and a secretary of state in the Abbasid caliphate, as being heavily in favor of music and its healthy effects, both spiritual and physical, al-Dhahabī tells us that music can be unlawful, reprehensible, permissible, recommended, and even religiously obligatory. The writer, as said before, comes from the extremely strict tradition of the Ḥanbalite school. The obligatory music is, of course, the Qur'an-recital (*tajwīd*), particularly when accompanied by an understanding of its meaning. The only unlawful and reprehensible forms of music are found where the singers are low-class ruffians performing with beautiful young girls who excite people's passions.[42] It is in this sense that the Pakistani poet-philosopher Muḥammad Iqbāl comments on al-Rūmī's verse about his musical instrument:

> The contemporary world, unstable and lacking in spiritual presence,
> Is intoxicated by low forms of music and can yield little spiritual pleasure.
> What does it know about this secret [of your music],
> What does it know about the Friend and His Voice?
> Alas! the West, with all its prosperity and its brilliance—
> Its music but drags it down into dust.[43]

Al-Dhahabī is also against music that brings on ecstasies (the aim of the Sufi) which take away men's senses. However, the author comes back to attack the extreme orthodox who would ban all music in favor of an ultra-puritanical and austere life-style à la Khomeini and says, "You should consider all this and do not hasten to declare unlawful where God has given people latitude and also forgiveness [for lapses]." Again,

> The Prophet—peace and blessings of God be upon him—brought an upright and straight faith that offers people latitude. He himself used to smile and laugh and had a sense of humor; he raced with his wife [ʿĀyisha] out of sport and carried his two little grandsons [al-Ḥasan and al-Ḥusain] sportily on his back and said, "What a nice man is your camel!" He played various kinds of sports. Where did peevishness, dry-facedness, and a frowning brow form part of his perfect character?[44]

·4·

Medical Care

There are a number of Ḥadīths exhorting the faithful to visit the sick and give them hope and comfort. "Visit the sick and free captives," the Prophet is reported to have said. Abū Huraira, a favorite companion of the Prophet, reported him as saying,

> God shall say on the Day of Judgment, "O son of Adam! I was sick but you did not visit me." "My Lord! how could I visit you when you are the Lord of the whole world," man will reply. God will say, "Did you not know that so and so from among my servants [that is, human beings] was sick but you never visited him or her? Did you not know that if you had visited, you would have found me there? O son of Adam! I was hungry but you did not feed me." "How could I feed you Lord! when you are the Lord of the world?" God shall answer, "Did you not know that so and so of my servants was hungry and asked you for food, but you did not feed him or her. Did you not know that if you had given food you would have found requital here?"[1]

According to one tradition, when the Prophet visited a sick person he would say, "No fear, it [illness] is a catharsis, God willing." People visiting the sick are asked to say such things to them as would make them happy; further, the Prophet encouraged visitors to request the sick person to pray for them because the state of the sick and the helpless is so pure that God hears their prayers." So, not only should the healthy pray for the recovery of the sick, but the sick may be profitably requested to do so for the healthy. God also visits the sick and says, "O my servant! health unites you with yourself, but sickness unites you to me."[2]

According to a Ḥadīth, the Prophet used to visit the sick after more than three days of illness. This Ḥadīth, of course, assumes correctly that because people were at home when they were sick (there were no hospitals in those days, in any case), for three days the sickness was taken to be ordinary—a cold or the like—but a longer period indicated that the sickness might be more serious. Sick people, as indeed healthy ones too, are strongly prohibited from desiring or praying for death, let alone committing suicide; for if a person is good, he may do more good if he lives longer, and if a person is not good, longer life may afford him a chance for conversion.[3] So far as possible, a sick person should not shout of pain or discomfort but try to be of good cheer.[4] 'Āyisha, the prophet's youngest wife, in whose lap he died, says that he experienced extreme discomfort at death; he constantly prayed to God to make his death easier; he had a utensil of water by his bedside, and he would frequently dip his hand in the water and cool his face with it. 'Āyisha says, "After witnessing the Prophet's [painful] death, I do not mind how much suffering anyone endures at death."[5] Al-Nawawī, the famous traditionist, is reported to have said that a dying person must hope for God's forgiveness and mercy and know that God is not keen to punish him: he should recite the Qur'anic verses and Ḥadīths from the Prophet that speak of hope and divine mercy.[6]

THE *AUQĀF* (PIOUS ENDOWMENTS)

Because health services in Islam (like other such charitable services as hospices, Sufi centers, mosques, and educational institutions) depended mostly on endowments, it is necessary to give a brief account of the law of *auqāf* before we go on to talk about health institutions and services supported by them. *Waqf*, plural *auqāf* (or *ḥabs*, plural *aḥbās* in North Africa; the official term there is *ḥabbūs*), literally means "to restrain" or "to stop," but in the Sharī'a law of Islam it is a technical term meaning "a pious or charitable endowment" because it restrains or confines a certain property to be used for certain charitable purposes. A *waqf* has to be made of wealth or durable property and is regarded as a contract between the *wāqif* (the person who makes the *waqf*) on the one side and God on the other: a competent judge (*qāḍī*) signs the contract on God's behalf —although it is not absolutely necessary for a *waqf*-contract to be written down and one can make such a contract by a public declaration. The person who makes an endowment must be of age (or be represented by a *walīy*, or guardian) and sane and must act of his or her own free will. The property to be made *waqf* must have been lawfully obtained or inherited. The purpose of the *waqf* must be good and charitable (*khair*), and it must not be intended for any evil design. Most Muslim jurists are of the opinion that *waqf* must be made in perpetuity and hence inalienably and that the endower forfeits all rights of ownership over the endowed property forthwith, although a small minority of them hold that a *waqf* may be withdrawn.

Trustees of such a charitable trust are charged with looking after it and seeing that the revenues are put to the best use in accordance with the terms set by the endower. An administrator or superintendent administers the *waqf*. A *waqf* can be for general charitable purposes—for the poor, widows, orphans, hospices—or it may be restricted for specific purposes laid down by the endower, in which case these wishes must be strictly adhered to unless impediments arise in realizing its stated objectives. In such cases it could be diverted to uses nearest to the endower's wishes and interests, or it could revert to the inheritors. In the history of Islam, governments have, from time to time, taken over the *auqāf* when they thought these were being maladministered or misused; generally the governments' aim was to increase revenues. There also arose in early Islam a kind of *waqf* or trust known as the "family trust" (*waqf 'ala' l-aulād*), which prevented the estate from being divided up into inheritance shares; it was kept intact and the revenues divided up among the inheritors. In most Muslim countries, a limit of thirty years has now been put on the duration of such trusts, after which time they must become subject to division by inheritance.

Except in the school of Mālik (d. 797 C.E.), Islamic law allows that the endower, and after him his inheritors, become the superintendent managers of the endowed property. Mālik's law says that once a person has executed an endowment, he or she has no role to play in the administration of the *waqf*. This explains why in the Maghrib (North Africa) and Muslim Spain, where Mālikī law prevailed, relatively few private endowments were made and therefore fewer privately endowed educational and health institutions existed,[7] although some great institutions were established by the rulers. In cases where the endower and the successors are not the administrators, a competent judge appoints them and also dismisses them for corruption or neglect of duty. The wages of the administrator but not those of the trustees come from the proceeds of the *waqf*. For mosques and mosque-schools, the *waqf* usually took the form of shops built around the mosque and then rented, which helped run the mosque and the school. Hospital *auqāf*, because of the large amount that had to be invested, usually required either a cash-endowment or a large piece of agricultural land from whose proceeds the hospital was run. Sufi lodges also were usually supported by land endowments, apart from individual offerings, especially those made by rich people as an act of piety or in gratitude for a curative prayer or prayer for birth of a son. To get some idea of the uses and abuses of this great institution in Islam (on the creation and regulation of which scores of books have been written by Muslim legists), the following brief quotation from W. Heffening's article in the *Encyclopaedia of Islam* is to the point:

> The waqf system in the east was very beneficial in ameliorating poverty and misery and in furthering learning [and, one might add, health], but it had its shady side morally as well as economically; on the one hand considerable sections of the populace were taken from industry by the continual injection of new sinecures and supported at the expense of the country; on the other hand, the capital for these great endowments had to be supplied by the wealthy and this was acquired not by productive labour but by extortion and unprecedented exploitation of the people (C. H. Becker, [*Islamstudien* 1:264ff.]). The immense accumulation of the landed property in the possession of the Dead Hand (that is, *auqāf*) further was economically injurious, although from time to time confiscations by the state and illegal disposal by the administrators had a regulating effect.[8]

According to Heffening, no precedent for the *waqf* institution existed in pre-Islamic Arabia, nor anything substantial in early Islam; he finds that the differences of opinion among the early legists about *waqf* suggest that "the institution of the *waqf* arose only after the death of the Prophet in the course of the first century A.H. [Islamic Era]. Its origin is to be sought in the strongly marked impulse to charitable deeds which is characteristic of Islam."[9] It is true that *waqf* and the laws governing it were developed by Muslims; however, its origins—besides, of course, the heavy emphasis the Qur'an places on socioeconomic justice and on "spending from the choicest parts of your wealth in the cause of Allah" and on the community and its weal—are connected with the pre-Islamic tribal institution of the *ḥimā*, land set apart by a tribe as communal property for grazing cattle and so on, which could not be claimed by any individual or family. It is also known that when, in 625 C.E., the Banu Naḍīr, a Jewish tribe of Medina, was exiled from there, accused of having sided with the opponents of Islam, the Meccans, in the battle of Uḥud, despite Jewish-Islamic cooperation agreements, their immobile property was made *waqf* for the benefit of the poor Muslims and was not distributed among Muslim individuals. Again, 'Umar I, the second caliph (d. 644), not only erected a huge *ḥimā* (for breeding horses for war) but against the general practice of the Prophet in peninsular Arabia, refused to distribute the lands of Iraq, after its conquest, among the Muslim soldiers as booty: instead, he made the whole territory a *waqf* on the Muslim community, from whose income shares were allotted to its members. These developments were directly relevant to the rise and rapid progress of the *waqf* institution in Islam.[10] This was quite apart from the *zakāt*—a tax levied on the well-to-do members of the community, collected in the public treasury (*bait al-māl*), and distributed among the poor and spent on works of public weal.

It should also be noted that the motivation behind these endowments was not always pure charity. It also protected the property from undue seizure by unscrupulous rulers and against emergencies (although, as said above, governments from time to time did seize them). It was also a means to avoid taxation and, of course, to save the patrimony from being divided up among heirs—it was a particularly effective weapon for excluding some heirs from inheritance. In some cases *waqf* was also used as a subterfuge for avoiding payments of debts, for not even a debtor could lay a claim to "Allah's property," although some legists did make *waqf* properties subject to debt deductions.[11]

At the present, in all Muslim countries, the *auqāf* have been taken over and administered by governments. In Turkey, they were abolished altogether by Mustafa Kemal the Ataturk in 1928. The extent of the *auqāf* lands can be gathered from the following:

> The estates of the Dead Hand in the former Turkish [Ottoman] Empire were estimated at three quarters of the whole arable land and in modern Turkey they have recently been calculated at Turkish £ 50,000,000 in value (1925); in the budget for the 1928 revenues are entered T.£. 3,489,000. Towards the middle of the sixteenth century, they comprised in Algiers one half, in 1883 in Tunis one third and in 1927 in Egypt one eighth of the cultivated soil. The accumulation of such extensive possessions in the Dead Hand meant a serious injury to the economic life of the country; but apart from anything else, a piece of ground that is waḳf [*waqf*] cannot be burdened by a mortgage.[12]

In the subcontinent of India also, *auqāf* were in great abundance. Al-Qalqashandī (d. 1418) writes on the authority of the Indian shaikh Mubārak al-Anbūtī (fourteenth century) that there were then in Delhi above one thousand schools and colleges (*madrasas*) and seven hundred hospitals as well as about two thousand Sufi lodges and hospices in and around Delhi,[13] all supported no doubt by *auqāf*. This is an extraordinary number of educational and health institutions and a particularly spectacular number of Sufi lodges and hospices. The kitchens of many of these lodges, particularly the large ones, were open to all and often functioned as hospices. Some Sufi orders in India, particularly the Chishtī order, with very few exceptions, did not accept immobile property as *waqf* but accepted only clothes, food, and other amenities that could be immediately distributed among the needy.[14]

The Sufis, in all Muslim lands, besides inducting and instructing their disciples in the Sufi Way, played sociopolitical roles. Politically, they were often mediators between the rulers and the masses in getting the latter's grievances redressed. In Ottoman Turkey, Sufis either led, or more often effectively participated in, almost all major rebellions against government. Because in Sunni Islam the religious scholars and doctors, the 'Ulama, are not as close to the masses as the Sufis, who often enjoyed tremendous popularity, rulers tried to win the Sufis' support; at the same time, they kept a watch on them because they were afraid of their tremendous potential power. The following two stories taken from the biography of a great Chishtī saint of Delhi, Shaikh Niẓām al-Dīn Auliyā' (d. 1325), illustrate more or less typically the Sufis' independent attitude toward the temporal power and their tremendous contributions to social service without regard for race or creed. The Khilji ruler 'Alā' al-Dīn sent a message to the shaikh inviting him to the court. The shaikh wrote back saying, "You are a great and powerful ruler, I am a *faqīr* [a word literally meaning "poor" but in Sufi terminology meaning "a Sufi" because they turned their backs on the pursuit of material life]; what is there in common between you and me to discuss?" and declined the invitation. The king then sent another message saying that if the shaikh could not come to the king's court, the king would come to the shaikh's lodge. The shaikh replied that since there was nothing in common between them to discuss, he did not understand why the king wanted to come, adding, "If you enter this lodge by the front door, I will leave by the back door." Later, the shaikh was summoned formally to appear in court because the 'Ulama charged him with indulging in music (*samā'*, which most Sufis practiced) while practicing his Sufi exercise. He went and spent a whole afternoon religiously defending his use of music; the king decided that there was nothing wrong with this practice. A stark contrast with the shaikh's attitude is offered by another story. One day, while on a walk outside his lodge, he saw a low-caste (*shūdra*) Hindu woman drawing water from a well. He asked her, "Why are you spending so much energy on drawing water from this well, while the river [Jumna] is flowing right by your side?" "We are very poor people," the woman replied, "the river water gives a lot of appetite, and we cannot afford much food, but the well water, being heavy, does not make one hungry." Upon his return to his lodge the shaikh ordered that at least so long as he was alive a tray of food must be sent daily to the poor woman's hut.[15]

This last story may well be true because it is in perfect harmony with whatever we know of Shaikh Niẓām al-Dīn. But even if it is not, it is genuinely symbolic of the Sufi attitude of general humanitarianism. This helps explain why so many *auqāf* were showered on the Sufis. It is obvious that the endowers of the *auqāf* were people of means who had something to endow, while the beneficiaries of these *auqāf* were either the Sufi shaikhs and their disciples or the poor people, who were either hungry or sick or needed food or shelter.

Before taking up the question of hospitals, a word may be in order concerning the *auqāf* specially concerned with hospitals. Although the following account cannot be taken literally as a rule for all hospital *auqāf*, which it is impossible to treat, it will, nevertheless give an indication of the concern for the correct application of *auqāf*-funds intended for hospitals. We are told that the directors/administrators of hospitals were usually men of high classes, some amirs or nobles. During the vizierate of 'Īsā ibn 'Alī, son of the aforementioned 'Alī ibn 'Īsā, the administrator of the *waqf*-endowment of the 'Aḍudī hospital, Abu'l-Ṣaqr, did not give enough money to the hospital. The reason was that since the endower, 'Aḍūd al-Daula, was a Shi'a, he had willed that a certain part of the funds be spent on the welfare of the Hashimites (the clan of the Prophet Muhammad) while the remaining sums be spent on the hospital. It seems that Abū'l- Ṣaqr began spending on the former item at the expense of the latter. Upon this, Thābit ibn Qurra, grandson of Thābit ibn Sinān, who was the hospital director, complained to the vizier 'Īsā ibn 'Alī who wrote to Abū'l-Ṣaqr:

> May God honor you! You know what has been mentioned [in Thābit ibn Qurra's letter of complaints]. . . . It is truly disgusting. Howsoever you may have manipulated matters concerning the increase of money [on the one side] and decrease [on the other] and made them more and less respectively, you must balance it out by taking from the other fund and putting it into the hospital fund. Indeed, the hospital is more deserving of these funds than other items because those who come to the hospital [for treatment] are helpless people and its benefit is very great. Please, let me know why hospital funds have fallen short for these successive months—particularly at this time of winter with such cold weather. Try every means at your disposal to relieve patients of the hardship and make haste to supply them with wheat, blankets, clothes, charcoal, and proper food, and their treatment and service must not be neglected. Inform me of what you have done [by way of restoration] and execute on my behalf such action as may satisfy me with your position and make the concern for the hospital your highest priority.[16]

HOSPITALS

The umayyad caliph al-Walīd (reg. 705–715) is said to have been the first to set up institutions for lepers and the blind where servants and guides were employed to help the inmates. But hospitals proper did not begin until the Abbasid caliphate (750–1257). Both the human initiative and the technical materials in the early period of their development came from the Gundaishāpūr college set up by the Sassanian ruler of Iran in 555.[17] The mainstay of the medical personnel were Nestorian Christians. It was the Christians, too, who shouldered the work of translating medical (and philosophical and other scientific) works from the Greek, often through the intermediary of Syriac, apart from some Indian Hindus who translated from Sanskrit works in medicine, mathematics, and astronomy. These translations were officially sponsored by the Abbasid caliph al-Ma'mūn, whose father, the illustrious Hārūn al-Rashīd, ordered the establishment of the first hospital at Baghdad. This hospital was set up by the Christian Jibrā'īl ibn Bakhtīshū', a doctor at Gundaishāpūr (descended from a family of doctors), who brought with him a dispensor as well. The son of this dispensor, a Persian Christian, Yuḥanna ibn Māsawaih, became eventually the head of this hospital. (The Persian term *bīmāristān*, "the place for the sick," was used for *hospital* by both the Arabs and later the Turks.) Hārūn's hospital was followed at the end of the ninth century by a number of new hospital foundations in quick succession, the first of these established by a page of the caliph al-Mu'taḍid (d. 902) and named for the caliph. 'Alī ibn 'Īsā, the "good vizier," founded a *bīmāristān* in 914 and appointed Abū 'Uthmān al-Dimashqī, a Christian who also made translations from the Greek, as the director of this hospital as well as of those in Mecca and Medina. He was succeeded as superintendent of these hospitals by the well-known physician, again a Christian, Sinān ibn Thābit, who himself set up a new hospital in 914.

Although many larger hospitals had quarters for mental patients, several hospitals were established specifically for them. Special homes were established also for orphans and old women. The same vizier, 'Alī ibn 'Īsā, ordered Sinān ibn Thābit to organize a team to visit the sick in jails. The letter reads:

> May God prolong your life! I have been thinking about prisoners, who, because of their overpopulation and the rugged conditions of their residence, must be frequent victims of diseases. But they are unable to pursue their own benefits and see doctors from whom they can seek advice about their health-afflictions. It is therefore behooving that you set apart some

> doctors to visit them daily; that medicines and medical drinks be carried to them; and that the doctors visit all prisoners and treat the sick.[18]

We are told that women paramedics accompanied the doctors.

Again, the same vizier ordered mobile dispensaries to be established to look after the health needs of the countryside, particularly surrounding the towns where no doctors were available. Sinān's son Thābit relates:

> A note came from the minister ['Alī ibn 'Īsā] to my father Sinān which said: "I have been thinking of the countryside of Sawād [southern Iraq] and the people who live there. There can be no doubt that there must be sick people whom no doctor looks after, because there are no doctors in the countryside. So go ahead—may God prolong your life—and send around doctors accompanied by medicines and liquid medical mixtures [potions]. They should go around the Sawād and stay in every part of it for so long a time as is needed and treat the sick therein and then move on to other parts." My father carried out these instructions.[18]

Certain doctors appear to have earned huge sums of money. Thus, the annual income of Jibrā'īl ibn Bakhtīshū' from his services to the caliph Hārūn, his viziers (the Barmakids), and other notables and from his landed estates, is recorded by his own secretary as being 4.9 million dirhams. His son Bakhtīshū' ibn Jibrā'īl, also a doctor, lived in high comfort: his chambers in his house at Baghdad were air-conditioned with ice in summer and charcoal in winter.[20] Many doctors are mentioned in the history of Islamic medicine who, from their income from medicine, set up their own hospitals and charitable clinics. Although great fortunes amassed by politicians like viziers and governors and military generals were, after their death, often liable to confiscation by the governments (called *muṣādara*) under the charge of appropriation of wealth by foul means, professionals like doctors were immune from this danger.[21]

Besides the hospitals and asylums, there were other types of health establishments. Special health centers were located near *jāmi*'s, the cathedral mosques where Friday services were held and where, therefore, large numbers of worshippers flocked. Army hospitals, with their own doctors and services, were often mobile because they followed the movements of the army. It is reported that the army of the Ghaznavid sultan Maḥmūd (d. 1030) was accompanied by a special medical caravan consisting of forty camels.[22]

But while caliphs and the nobles and special groups were well served by their physicians, the number of other hospitals in cities and provincial towns also grew, and new hospitals grew larger and more comprehensive. The Aḍudī hospital set up in Baghdad in 982 by the Būyid ʿAḍud al-Daula (d. 983) became the most famous of the early hospitals. Abū-Bakr al-Rāzī is generally mentioned as having been chosen as its administrator from among a hundred names;[23] he is said to have selected the site at the banks of the river Tigris after hanging a piece of meat in several places for a few days and deciding in favor of the place where meat was found to be least infected. When first founded, this hospital had twenty-four doctors with different specializations. A doctor who did his duty two days and two nights a week is said to have been paid three hundred dirhams per month.

Nūr al-Dīn ibn Zanji (d. 1175) built a famous hospital in Damascus. The medical historian Ibn Abī Uṣaibiʿa describes the routine works of this hospital:

> When the just ruler Nūr al-Dīn created the great hospital, he entrusted the medical side of it to Abū'l Majd ibn Abī'l-Ḥakam. . . . Abū'l Majd used to make rounds investigating the patients' conditions. With him were supervisors and the personnel that served the patients. Records were kept for every patient—the medicines, food, and other treatment plans prescribed. No delay occurred in carrying out these instructions. After these rounds and his visit to the castle, where he examined and treated the high officials, he returned to the hospital, sat in its large carpeted quadrangle, and occupied himself with the study of his books. Nūr al-Dīn himself had dedicated a large number of medical books to the hospital. A group of doctors and apprentices [the equivalents of modern residents] used to come and sit in front of him carrying on discussions. He also lectured to students. He was occupied with this for a period of three hours, at the end of which he left for home.
>
> All patients were first examined in the outer hall. Those who were not seriously ill were given medicines and sent home; those with more serious ailments were admitted to the hospital. They were bathed and given new clothes. Their old clothes were sent to the storage. After discharge, they were given new clothes and a certain amount of money. The well-known doctor and traveler ʿAbd al-Laṭīf al-Baghdādī (d. 1238), who also taught at Damascus, narrates an amusing story of an intelligent Persian youth who was tempted by the excellent food and service of the Nūrī hospital and pretended to be sick. A doctor examined him and at once came to know the real intention of the young man. He admitted him and gave him excellent food for three days, after which he said to him, "Arab hospitality lasts for three days; please go home now."[24]

A fairly typical picture of the teaching and medical practice in a high-ranking hospital appears in this account by the historian Ibn Abī Uṣaibiʿa

(d. 1270), whose *'Uyūn al-Anbā' 'an Ṭabaqāt al-Aṭibbā'* (The Sources of Information concerning the Classes of Doctors) is the most important source for the history of Islamic medicine:

> When Shaikh Muhadhdhab al-Dīn came to stay at Damascus, he began to teach medicine. A large number of prominent doctors and others swarmed around him to study with him, and I too stayed in Damascus to study with him. First I had studied with him in the army where my father and doctor Muhadhdhab al-Dīn were serving the great [Ayyūbid] sultan. After he started teaching [presumably in the Nūrī Medical Collegeı, I kept going to him along with a group of others and started reading the works of Galen; he was thoroughly well versed in the books we read with him by Galen and others. He was eloquent, had an excellent ability to communicate ideas, and was a superior discussant. I also worked with him during his clinic hours at the hospital; I gained good practical knowledge there also and participated in the practice of the medical art.
>
> Contemporary with him in the work of the treatment of patients at the hospital was the *Ḥakīm* [doctor] 'Imrān, one of the foremost experts in the art of healing with expertise in a wide range of therapeutic areas. From the presence of these two men, I acquired double benefits—particularly from the discussions that went on between the two concerning diseases and their treatments and their advice and instructions to patients. . . .
>
> There was also in the hospital at the time Shaikh Raḍīy al-Dīn al-Raḥbī, one of the senior doctors in years and the greatest of them in respect and the most famous of them. He used to sit on a [carpeted] dais and write for visiting patients—after they described to him their ailments—prescriptions on the basis of which they got medicines and potions. Having accompanied doctors Muhadhdhab al-Dīn and 'Imrān, who treated inpatients in the hospital, I used to sit with Doctor Raḍīy al Dīn al-Raḥbī after the first two finished their work and watch his argumentation about diseases, his advice to patients, and what he prescribed for them. I discussed with him many diseases and their treatment.
>
> Ever since this hospital was created [by Nūr alīn ibn Zanji], there never gathered together at one time—nor ever thereafter—such preeminent medical authorities as happened at that time by the coming together of these three. This lasted for a good while—and
>
> Then those years and those who lived through them all passed away,
> It's as though those years and those men are no more than dreams![25]

The largest and the greatest hospital built in Egypt was the Manṣūrī, built by the Mameluke ruler of Egypt Manṣūr Qalā'ūn in Cairo and completed in 1284. The annual income from the endowment of this most elaborate hospital in Islam was about one million dirhams. It is said that Qalā'ūn, when on a visit to Syria, was taken ill with colic and was treated in the Nūrī hospital in Damascus. He was so pleased and impressed with both the hospital and his successful treatment that he vowed to build a hospital in Cairo. Men and women were admitted in separate wards. Nobody, irrespective of race, creed, and sex, was turned away, nor was the period of stay as an inpatient limited. This hospital was converted (as was the earlier Nāṣirī hospital in Cairo established by Ṣalāḥ al-Dīn al-Ayyūbī [Saladin]) from a large palace which had the capacity for accommodating eight thousand people. The Manṣūrī possessed wards equipped for the treatment of things as diverse as fever and eye diseases as well as for internal medicine and surgery. It had a pharmacy, as did many other large hospitals, and male and female attendants; besides lecture rooms, it had a rich library. It also had a chapel for Christians and a mosque for Muslims. Part of the *waqf*-document of the Manṣūrī reads:

> As for the above-mentioned hospital founded by our master, the said sultan—he has dedicated it as a place of medical treatment for Muslim patients, male or female, rich and poor, from Cairo and the countryside of Egypt. Both residents and nonresidents from other countries, no matter what their race, religion, and so on, [shall be treated here] for their ailments, big or small, similar or different, whether the diseases are perceptible [that is, are physical] or whether they are mental disturbances, because the preservation of mental order is one of the basic aims of the Sharī'a [in Islamic law, five "fundamental rights" are to be guaranteed to all citizens: preservation of life, religion, property, personal honor (*'irḍ*), and sound mind (*aql*)]. *The foremost attention* [*in law*] *is to be paid to those who have suffered loss of mind and hence loss of honor.* These and other maladies it is needful to treat through compound medicines or simple ones, which are well-known to those who are versed in the art of medicine and practice it. Single people shall be admitted to it as well as whole groups, whether they are old or young, children or women. The hospital shall keep all patients, men and women, for treatment until they are completely recovered. All costs are to be borne by the hospital whether the people come from afar or near, whether they are residents or foreigners, strong or weak, low or high, rich or poor, the employed and the employers [that is, of all social classes], blind or sighted, famed or obscure, learned or illiterate. There are no conditions of consideration and payment; none is objected to or even indirectly hinted at from nonpayment. The entire service is through the magnificence of God, the generous one.[26]

It is noteworthy that while the benefactor sultan is mentioned early in the *waqf*-deed, the document ends by praising the magnificence of God alone.

The hospital is still in use and since 1915 has been specializing in the treatment of blind people.

We also hear that in certain hospitals music was played for the patients. When Sultan al-Nāṣir built a hospital in Mayyā Fariqīn (now in southeastern Turkey but at that time part of Ayyūbid Syria), musicians and singers were regularly sent to console and cheer patients. This is all the more striking in face of the ban on music by the Islamic orthodoxy from very early times. Despite this ban, however, music was quite widespread at rulers' courts and nobles' homes and at various popular mass-gatherings. The Sufis, of course, used music in their mystical exercises. In the contemporary Muslim world, Ayatollah Khomeini banned music after his takeover of power in Iran in 1979, except military music. According to the *Seyāhatnāme* (Book of Travels) of Evliyā Çelebī, the seventeenth-century Ottoman litterateur, scholar, and traveler, who has described several hospitals in the Ottoman empire, music was used in the hospital built by the sultan Muhammad the Conqueror in Istanbul. In the hospital built by Sultan Bāyezid II in Edirne, a staff of ten musicians regularly played music and sang to patients. According to Çelebī, music was also used in some hospitals of Damascus (apparently built by the Ottoman government). Music, then, was a more or less regular feature of treatment. It was used especially for the mentally sick, although for the entertainment of general patients as well.[27] In his *Turkish Medical History during Five-and-a-Half Centuries*, Osman Ševki devotes a section to music therapy. He claims first that it was the Arabs who had derived certain conclusions from the practice of music in the hospital at Madā'in and had made music and musical instruments for sick persons, depressed patients, and mad patients who had to be kept in chains. He also claims, on the authority of a work by the Turkish doctor Shu'ūrī, *Balance of Temperaments*, that Turkish doctors had derived ideas about various types of music and dance from the rate and rhythm of the pulse. According to the unanimous tradition of Muslim historians, al-Fārābī (d. 950), the great philosopher, medical savant, and musician, constructed a musical instrument which he played at the court of his patron prince Saif al-Daula and whose various tunes were particularly effective in arousing different emotions.[28]

A word must also be said about physical conditions in many of these hospitals, especially those established by rulers, princes, and nobles. Some of these—in Cairo and Damascus—were palaces turned into hospitals. Several accounts of their luxurious furniture exist as well. Although accounts of highly expensive beddings and clothing may well be regarded as poetic exaggerations when given by a literary figure like Evilyā Çelebī, more reliable sources also tell of Baghdad hospitals whose luxurious furniture and furnishings "were no different from those of princes' palaces."[29] There is little doubt that such furnishings were inspired by the Islamic teaching about the general welfare of the poor and specifically about care of ill people. The Qur'an itself is eloquent on the point: "You shall not attain to virtue unless you spend [for the welfare of the poor] from the choicest part of your wealth" (3, 92); "O You who believe! spend [for the poor] from the worthiest part of [the wealth] you have earned and your crop-yields, and do not give away from its unworthy parts—such that you yourselves will not take until you examine [its quality] minutely—and know that God is not in your need and all praise belongs to Him" (2, 267). Verse 2, 266 cites an effective parable: "Would any of you want that he possess a garden of palms and grapes beneath which water-conduits flow and which yields all sorts of fruit, but when he reaches old age and still has small and weak children, the garden is struck with stormy downpours containing lightning and is all burnt out?"

Finally, there seems to have been some practice in these hospitals of allowing the patients' relatives to be present, at least in serious cases, as is brought out by the following story:

> Ibn al-Maṭrān relates that a patient was suffering [in the Cairo hospital set up by Ṣalāḥ al-Dīn al-Ayyūbī) from ascitic dropsy, and he wanted to puncture it. At that time there was in the hospital Ibn Hamdān, the surgeon. So they both decided upon the operation. The operation was done, and yellow fluid began to flow. Ibn al-Maṭrān kept his hand on the patient's pulse, and when he found that the patient's strength was failing and he could not let out more fluid, he stopped the flow and sewed up the spot. He told the patient's wife, when leaving, that under no condition must she let him open the wound or remove the bandage until he visited him the next day. When he left and the night came, the man said to his wife, "I feel much better and the doctor has sewn my wound up for no better reason than to postpone my recovery. Please remove the band so that all the fluid gets out and I go about my work." She refused, but he kept insisting. . . . Finally, she removed the bandage, the entire fluid went out; he lost all strength and died.[30]

MEDICAL CLINICS

The account of hospitals and their operations in the central lands of Islam holds true of Persia as well during the classical age of medicine, for men of preeminence in the medical field like al-Rāzī and Ibn Sīnā were Persians. But whereas the tradition of hospitals in the Arab lands and in the Ottoman empire continued into the present, little is heard of them in Iran, at least after the advent of the Safavid dynasty in the fifteenth century. In India, although contacts of medical men with the Islamic Middle East had begun in the early Abbasid period, when al-Bīrunī visited India in the company of the conquering army of Maḥmūd Ghaznavī toward the end of the tenth century, Islamic medicine had not yet gained a large foothold. This did not happen until after, and indeed as a consequence of, Mongol invasion of Baghdad and Iran in the thirteenth century, which drove scholars and doctors of eminence into India. There is evidence that during the reign of 'Alā' al-Dīn Khilji (d.1321), teaching of medicine in Arabic was fairly well established. The Indian Muslim king Muḥammad ibn Tughlaq (d. 1352) and his successor Fīrūz Shāh Tughlaq (d. 1388) were both doctors. The latter is reported to have "built five additional hospitals," one of which has received prominent mention by historians. This hospital at Delhi had a large staff of doctors and paramedics and had all the medicines and food for patients. Medicines were arranged and registered according to ailments "from head to foot" as was often the case in descriptions of diseases and their treatments in medical works. Patients stayed in the hospital until they recovered and then returned home "after offering prayers for the king." Treatment, drugs, and food were all free. The king himself visited the hospital from time to time and personally treated patients. He was especially interested in ophthalmology and prepared an effective collyrium from the skin of black snakes known as "Fīrūzshāhī collyrium" which is still used. He also wrote a medical work titled "Fīrūzshāhī Medicine." Shēr Shāh Sūrī, who ruled India from 1544 to 1549, built roads (particularly the famous Grand Trunk Road from Delhi to the northwestern frontier of India) and dug wells for travelers, also built for travelers numerous hospices "with a hospital attached to each hospice." The Mogul emperor Jehāngīr, according to his Institute Number 8, established hospitals within the chief cities of his realm, appointed physicians to attend the sick, and directed that expenses be defrayed from the royal treasury."[31] In many of these hospitals both Muslim *ṭabībs* and Hindu *veds* were appointed (because Hindus would not have themselves treated by non-Hindus), as also in the important hospital established and endowed by Nawwāb Khair-Andīsh Khān Karbā at Itāwa during Aurangzīb 'Ālamgīr's reign.[32] A big hospital was established in 1595 at Hyderabad, India, whose building can still be seen today.[33]

It appears, however, that these "hospitals" were mostly clinics. Doctors (now most often called *ḥakīms* or wise men, rather than *ṭabībs*) either were attached to courts of rulers, governors, and other potentates and received large salaries or were endowed wealth and particularly fiefs to set up charitable dispensaries for the poor and make house calls for those more seriously ill. Why clinics rather than hospitals developed is not clear; no obvious economic or political reasons adequately explain it. It is correct that medical standards fell after the Mongol invasion, and a marked decline had occurred by the fifteenth-sixteenth centuries, although some remarkably able doctors continued to arise both in Iran and in India. Medicine underwent a tremendous expansion and consequent vulgarization: one could find some doctor, no matter how ill-trained, in practically every village. Medical education became, with the advent of the Seljūk Turks, a part of the general Islamic education, and every person who had *some* education also knew *some* medicine. But medicine is not the only science that declined in later medieval Islamic centuries—all sciences, even religious sciences, declined; so vulgarization cannot be the whole explanation for the deterioration of medicine.

The clinical experience, of course, grew and was often written down and compiled by clinicians in their works. This literature, called *al-mujarrabāt* (treatments based on repeated experience), is surely scientific at its core, although it is the result not of *controlled experimentation* but of *experience.* It is true that at times "superstition," amulets, for example, did find a place in this literature, but even what we may call "superstitious" had a definite psychological/spiritual curative function. The *mujarrabāt* literature grew with the expansion of clinical medicine. The most famous doctor of Safavid Iran, Bahā' al-Daula (d.1507), wrote a book titled *The Quintessence of Experience* (*Khulāṣat al-Tajārib*), about which Cyril Elgood says, "This work combines the clinical acumen and personal touches of the *Continens* [that is, *al-Ḥāwī* of al-Rāzī] with the orderly presentation of the *Canon* [that is, *al-Qānūn* of Ibn Sīnā]. It is essentially practical, yet full of original observations and aphorisms."[34]

Elgood further says of Bahā' al-Daula, "He was the first to record (as far as I know) the spontaneous cure of *cutaneous Leishmaniasis* after twelve months of ulceration. In his chapter on eruptive fevers he describes three diseases which he says passed unnoticed up to his time, which, though resembling them, are neither smallpox nor measles. He makes one wonder whether he was not describing chicken pox, German measles, and the Fourth Disease." Elgood continues, "His description of an epidemic cough, which occurred at Herat while he was there, can be nothing else but the earliest account of whooping cough. This disease was not recognized in Europe until the end of the sixteenth century and was not described until Willi wrote his monograph in 1674." Certainly, this literature contains some generalized observations which are often no more than educated guesses. Thus, Elgood says, "Bahā' al-Daula asserts that stammerers never become bald, that a black and lustreless pupil in a state of health signifies a short life, that as long as a splenomegalic complains of pain in the left side there is a hope of a cure, that a fruit eater is very prone to catarrh, and that the appearance of pigmentary patches on the face or body of an epileptic heralds the cessation of fits."[35] These are, however, observations and can hardly be characterized as magical statements, as critics like Ullmann have maintained.[36]

In the Indian subcontinent, Muslim *ṭabībs* also combined with the traditional Islamic medicine the traditional Hindu medicine called the Ayurvedic —in fact, almost completely absorbing it. Particularly, and, indeed, naturally, this was the case with pharmacology because many herbs found in India were not found in the Middle East or even Iran. The courts of rulers were attended by both Muslim and Hindu doctors. Akbar's court had a combined team of twenty-nine doctors from both traditions.[37] The patronage of Islamic medicine by the sultans, nobles, governors, and other potentates was very widespread indeed. Even in villages, thanks to the teaching of some medicine as a part of the normal religious curriculum in the *madrasas*, the *imam* of a mosque was usually also a doctor, no matter how ill-equipped he might be. Hospitals were usually found in large towns and cities, to which journeys were taken by patients just as they journeyed to shrines, but small outpatient clinics were usually quite near, and often at hand. Although in the absence of elaborate hospitals it was naturally difficult to treat complicated diseases, the abundance of relatively small clinics, spread all over, treated and saved many sick people who did not have rare or complicated diseases. Hence, while the absence of large hospitals made for the decline of medicine *as a science*, its benefits *as a practical art* increased simply because treatment was available to a much larger body of people.

Indian medical men have made several contributions to medical literature both in Arabic and Persian; this literature consists of either commentaries on the classical medical works of Islam, like *The Canon* of Ibn Sīnā or the *Nafīsī* of Ibn al-Nafīs or compilations of which the *mujarrabāt* form a prominent part. That these compilations were extremely common—a sort of medical recipe literature—is also shown by the travels of the French "doctor" Bernier, who was in India during the time of the Mogul rulers Shāh Jehān and Aurangzīb (seventeenth century). He writes about Hindus that their current medical literature consisted exclusively of actual prescriptions. It is possible that this development on such a large scale among Muslims was also influenced by Hindus. Bernier further writes that Hindus would have nothing whatever to do with anatomy even of animals.[38]

The contemporary Ḥakīm 'Alī Aḥmad Nayyir Wāsiṭī, in his Urdu translation, commentary, and critique of Browne's *Arabian Medicine* (*Ṭibb al-'Arab*), writes about a late Mogul *ḥakīm*, Sharīf Khān (who had produced a massive synthesis of the Hindu Ayurvedic system of medicine with that of the *yūnānī* medicine),

> In the later history of [Islamic] medicine, Ḥakīm Sharīf Khān deserves special mention. He was a highly learned and skillful doctor of the reign of the [Mogul] Muḥammad Shāh. He wrote commentaries on Ibn al-Nafīs's commentary on *The Canon* (this most probably refers to Ibn al-Nafīs's projected hundred-volume work on medicine, of which he is reported to have completed only thirty and of which some are known to have survived) and *Sharḥ al-Asbāb* (causes of different maladies), from which one can form an idea of the vastness and depth of his knowledge. He wrote a work on simple medicines (*mafradāt*) titled *Ta'līf-i Sharīfī* and, on compound medicines, another work wherein he deposited the *mujarrabāt* and *ma'mūlāt* (prescriptions proven by experience and relied upon as cures) of his ancestors (as well as his own) and which he titled *'Ilāj al-Amrāḍ* (Cure of Maladies).

Similarly, "during the reign of Farrukh Siyar, Ḥakīm Muḥammad Akbar Arzāni [an emigrant from Iran] wrote a medical dictionary titled *Ḥudūd al-Amrāḍ* (Definitions of Diseases), and in practical medicine two separate books called *Mīzān al-Ṭibb* (The Scale of Medicine) and *Ṭibb-i Akbar* (The Greater Medicine)";[39] these last two, no doubt, constitute the *mujarrabāt*. There are many other works titled *al-Mujarrabāt*; for example, one appears among the list of works of a prominent doctor, 'Alī Jīlānī, who came from Iran during Akbar's reign and was his court physician.

The Tughlaq king of India, Fīrūz Shāh (d.1388) and the "Great Mogul" emperor Akbar both are said by historians to have learned medicine and treated patients, the former having done it as a rule in a hospital built by him while the latter treated certain of his courtiers, including the well-known Amīr 'Abd al-Raḥīm Khān-i Khānān. The following anecdote about the fatal illness of Akbar sheds some light on the privileges and risks of royal physicians and the court intrigues. Akbar's son and successor Jehāngīr writes in his autobiography:

> In 1016 [1606 C.E.], my father used to eat many kinds of food and fruits, while his illness had taken a serious turn, simply to please his relatives and

> friends [who offered him such food], and because he was weak due to old age, he could not digest them. One day he became very angry with Amīn al-Daula, who would not cease from gambling. His anger made him still more weak and ill. He developed dysentery and could eat nothing. The same was the case Tuesday [the next day]. On Wednesday, he was advised to take some soup. One day, the king became somewhat angry with his [official] doctor 'Ali Jīlānī [for not being able to cure him]. This doctor himself used to spend six thousand rupees annually on the treatment of the poor. The doctor said, "The treatment that I have prescribed is good, provided it agrees with you. But you do not help yourself and do not avoid things I ask you to avoid. You were sent kedgerie (*khichrī*, a dish prepared with rice, butter, and a heavy lentil called *māsh*) from your wives' quarters and you ate it with zest. It proved too heavy for you to digest and you have started to have diarrhea."

Akbar's diarrhea soon changed into dysentery. A chronicler writes:

> Toward the end, when Akbar began to pass blood in his stools and the doctor 'Ali Jīlānī could do nothing, the king burst upon him in anger and said, "You were an ordinary man but I raised you to this high rank. When will you prove of any use to me, after all?" The king was so angry that he took off his belt and waved it toward the doctor. The doctor took out a medicine from his pocket and put it into a glass of water. The water froze instantaneously. The doctor said, "Such medicines do exist [as might stop your diarrhea], but what can I do when nothing seems to work?" The king said, "Whatever is to happen will happen, but please let me have this medicine." The doctor would not refuse and administered him the medicine. The result was a binding constipation, a swollen stomach, and intense spasms in the stomach. The doctor found himself compelled to give antidotes which brought back diarrhea resulting in the patient's death. The doctor was so frightened that he took refuge with Shaikh Farīd [the governor of Lahore].

The doctor had reason to be frightened because other doctors were accusing him of not treating the king correctly. Particularly, another co-doctor, Muẓaffar, objected to 'Ali Jīlānī's prescribing watermelon for the king during illness. Emperor Jehāngīr writes in his autobiography: "Doctor Muẓaffar told me that the administration of watermelon to the king at the beginning of his illness was a big mistake. But I used my good sense and thought that whether doctor Muẓaffar was speaking truthfully or out of malice and selfishness, I would not make doctor Jīlānī a target of my wrath by reading any evil intention into his mind. But for God's decree and doctors' mistakes, who would ever die?"[40] The death of Akbar did arouse suspicions of foul play in his treatment because Sunni Muslims were against the emperor's religious policies and beliefs: his extratolerant attitude toward the Hindus, his adoption of certain Hindu and, indeed, Zoroastrian practices, his flirting with certain Catholic emissaries of the Pope, and his eclectic court religion. Already before his death, their representatives had approached his son Jehāngīr, pledging him support for the throne against his rival if he would reintroduce orthodox Islamic policies, which he is said to have agreed to, while many Hindus (Rāja Mān Singh in particular—Akbar's army commander, father-in-law, and a prominent courtier, who nevertheless refused to accept Akbar's religion) and some Muslims preferred to see on the throne Jehāngīr's son, Prince Khusro. No real evidence of any foul play, has, however, been substantiated.

This case of a monarch's treatment is not atypical in either its medical or political aspect, although in Akbar's case this latter was accentuated because of the important religious factor involved. The treatment of a commoner, a poor and blind woman, provides another case. I have spoken of the vast spread of clinics in Islamic India under the patronage of powerful and rich persons, where treatment was free for the poor. The case we are now going to narrate is, therefore, not rare either, except that, as sometimes happened, high personages themselves got involved if cases of poor people came to their personal notice. The last great Mogul emperor Aurangzīb 'Ālamgīr (d.1707) was camping at Wah Gardens not far from where now lies Islamabad, the capital of Pakistan. His court historian, Musta'id Khan (d.1724), who accompanied the emperor, tells us in his *Ma'āthir-i 'Ālamgīrī* (History of 'Ālamgīr's Reign):

> One day my personal servants told me that just by the side of the royal camp there lives a blind old woman who works a flour mill which operates on the water that comes from the garden and falls into a stream. Because the park superintendent has stopped this water [it is not mentioned for what reason], the woman has lost her livelihood and we cannot get flour to make bread for ourselves. Musta'id Khan conveyed this message to the emperor through Bakhtāwar Khan, a confidant and high official of 'Ālamgīr, who was ordered to get the water flowing again under the woman's flour mill. When 'Ālamgīr sat down to his meal, he ordered two trays of food and five gold coins to be sent to the woman with a message of greeting saying, "You are our neighbor. I am sorry that my stay here has caused you harassment; please forgive me." The next day the emperor sent a palanquin for the woman, who was brought to the palace. On inquiring from her he found that she was a widow with two unmarried daughters and two small sons. She was given two hundred rupees and stayed in the camp palace for two nights, where women of the royal household generously gave her clothes and jewelry. Two or three days later the woman was again invited into the royal camp along with her

> daughters. This time she received two thousand rupees, clothes, and jewelry for her daughters. She was also given an additional mill, and both of her mills were made tax-exempt. She married her daughters off; she became very well-off and could provide her half-naked sons with good clothes. Musta'id Khan said that when she came to see him in order to thank him, she was wearing gold-embroidered shoes and was loaded with jewelry. To top it all, her blindness was cured by an ophthalmologist, Doctor Subhān, under orders from the emperor.[41]

I have given this story in detail and have not been content with stating that a blind old woman was treated by a king's order because the attitude of mind behind this event is absolutely important: the curing of the woman's blindness is an inalienable part of a whole *attitude of caring* in which 'Ālamgīr is by no means unique in the history of Indian Islam.

Two women in the Mogul period are spoken of as possessing knowledge of medicine and also using it occasionally although probably not practicing it. One is an Iranian woman named Satīy al-Nisā', whose brother Ṭālib was a poet of note at the court of the Mogul emperor Shāh Jehān. She came to India from Iran fourteen years after her brother. She is said to have become an important personage in the palace because of her skill in general house-management and her exceptional ability at nursing (*tīmārdārī*) and also treating patients among palace servants. She also became the keeper of the seal for Shāh Jehān's beloved wife Mumtāz Maḥal, for whom the king built the famous Tāj Maḥal; she also tutored Mumtāz Maḥal's daughter Jehān Ārā. She died in 1646 in Lahore, where she was first buried, but the emperor constructed a magnificent mausoleum by the side of the great Tāj Maḥal, and her body was interred there a year and some months after her death.[42]

The second lady is Nūr Jehān, Jehāngīr's beloved wife about whom he writes in his autobiography, "she was more medically experienced than these doctors." This he writes in connection with his bitter complaints against his two well-known court physicians, Abū'l-Qāsim Jīlānī and Ṣadr al-Dīn. They were with him on his Kashmir campaign in 1621 when he developed severe edema (it seems to have been common among the males of the royal families, possibly because of high cholesterol diets) and breathing trouble, but both refused to treat him. Jehāngīr writes that despite the fact that he had treated them so well in giving them high ranks, they callously refused to treat him. It has been suggested that because of a grim struggle for succession, these two were afraid to touch the king in this condition. Both were suspected of harboring feelings for his son Shāh Jehān, who actually succeeded him and in whose reign both of them became prominent favorites. What is amazing, however, is that he took no action against them. There are no details of how Nūr Jehān treated her husband except that she decreased his very high consumption of alcohol and kept him on a strict diet.[43]

It is not surprising that the two women knew something about medicine because medicine had become part of the normal education. While most middle-class educated women probably only studied some Qur'an and the Prophetic traditions and a certain amount of the Sacred Law that was particularly relevant to women, palace women and other women of nobility undoubtedly learned much more, including literature and medicine. That hygiene and medicine had become part of general knowledge is clear from the career of a well-known book titled *Bihishtī Zewar* (Jewelry of Paradise), written by a famous Indian religious scholar, Ashraf 'Alī Thānavī (d. 1943), as advice for women concerning religion and general well-being. The first edition of this book appeared in the early 1880s, but since then it has undergone countless editions. Every new edition became larger and larger until by 1942, slightly before the author's death, it had swollen to forty-four volumes. It was, and even with the spread of modern education still is —particularly among the conservative strata of society—the custom that whenever Muslim girls are wed, they bring from their parents' home this book as part of their dower. The work seeks to provide a complete guide for life; apart from religious instruction, it has substantial portions devoted to cookery, the hygienic importance of clean linen, medical prescriptions for numerous ailments, even instructions on what clothes to wear when the wind blows from the north or south. Covering about six decades of history with ever new additions, the work has a first-rate sociological importance.[44]

MEDICAL EDUCATION AND MEDICAL EXAMINATION

Medical education in Islam began as a function of large hospitals: all large hospitals like that founded by 'Aḍūd al-Daula in the latter half of the tenth century in Baghdad were teaching hospitals. The account given above from Ibn Abī Uṣaibi'a, the historian of medicine, detailed his medical education at the Nūrī hospital in Damascus and also revealed the manner in which teaching and clinical research were conducted. This was in all probability taken over from the medical tradition of Gundaishāpūr, which had first inspired and guided the founding of hospitals in Baghdad. These professional schools ran parallel with the development of institutions of religious learning called *madrasas*, the important difference being that whereas the *madrasas* started out as private foundations, the medical institutions were established under official sponsorship. The first state-sponsored *madrasas* were established in Sunni Islam in the eleventh century, under the Seljūk Turks: Niẓām al-Mulk, the "wise" minister of the Seljūk rulers, founded in 1063–65 the famous Niẓāmīya College at Baghdad. The motivations behind this development seem to have been two: first, to counteract the Shi'a propaganda (the Shi'a had preceded the Sunnis in establishing seats of learning under official aegis—the great seminary of al-Azhar at Cairo was founded and run by the Shi'a Fatimids in 970 until it was taken over by the Sunni Ayyūbids in 1176), and second, to produce state officials for the administration of Islamic institutions (prior to the Seljūkids there was no special official in charge of Islam; it was the Turks who created the high office of the Shaikh al-Islām).

As was the case with Islamic learning, so in the field of medicine too, students usually sought out great masters with whom to study, and the importance of the institutions was only secondary. After a student learned certain subjects, both on the basis of books and clinical experience with a master, the master, and not the institution, gave him the *ijāza*, the certificate that enabled him to teach or practice precisely those subjects. In order to study with a famous master, the fame of whose expertise had spread far and wide, students would travel from all corners of the Muslim world. It was quite common for an ambitious student to study, for example, ophthalmology with a master in Cairo and then move on to Damascus or Baghdad to study diseases of the kidney.

After the *madrasas* began to be established under official patronage, medical sciences were also gradually made a part. Physicians, of course, had been turned out in large numbers by earlier medical institutions: a system of testing doctors was instituted in the thirties of the tenth century. We are told that when doctors were first asked to submit themselves to examination before practicing medicine, a process directed by Sinān ibn Thābit, Baghdad alone had 860 doctors, excluding court doctors who were not required to take the exam.[45] But after medicine became an optional part of the integral religious studies curriculum, the number of doctors multiplied still further. The building of the famous Mustanṣirīya *madrasa* at Baghdad, which still operates today, was established by the Abbasid caliph al-Mustanṣir-Bi'llāh; it was completed in 1233, but in 1234 the medical section was added with its own building.[46] The Ottoman sultan Muhammad the conqueror (Mehmet Fātih) built in Istanbul, after its conquest, a large *madrasa* with a sixteen-year curriculum. At the apex, students specialized in one of two faculties, that of religion and that of natural sciences. The first consisted of departments of theology, law, and literature; the second comprised the departments of natural science, philosophy, and medicine. This also seems to have been the case with the *madrasa* of the sultan Sulaimān the Magnificent (or Sulaimān the Law-Giver, d. 1566).[47]

In the Indian subcontinent, too, *yūnānī* medicine (Ionian or Greek medicine) was taught as a regular subject in the large *madrasas*, while practical training was acquired in the clinics spread all over India. Because medicine had, by the time of the Moguls, become part of religious teaching, "in the Mogul period, medicine was generally taught . . . in the *madrasas* and places of religious learning. It is for this reason that we find that, in this period, practically all men learned in religion were also well-versed in medicine. In addition, practical training was given by experts in their clinics . . . and it was these [clinics] which were the real medical schools."[48]

The immediate cause of the institution of doctors' exams is said to have been the sensational death in 931 of a patient in a Baghdad hospital. We are told that out of the 860 medical practitioners in Baghdad 160 failed. It is clear that the exam was rather lenient and that its purpose was more to save people from dangerous quacks than to standardize the quality of practitioners. E. G. Browne quotes an amusing story of an impressive and well-dressed elderly gentleman and his son who knew nothing of medicine except certain laxatives but said they made enough money by prescribing these harmless medicines. Sinān ibn Thābit let them carry on their business provided that they did not go beyond these.[49]

The supervision of doctors and their practice was eventually given over to the department of *Ḥisba* (the Arabic *ḥisāb* means to take account of, to examine, or to judge), which was charged with the task of looking after "public morality"—checking weights and measures, examining the quality of commodities, and investigating charges of drunkenness, professional fraud, and so on. Consequently, this function became part of the *Ḥisba* in all major towns. The strictness of the application of standards, however, varied with time, place, and personnel. In the Arab Middle East, we hear of such exams being established in Baghdad, Cairo, and Damascus. According to the Arab historian Jurjī Zaidān, there was an office of "chief physician" in Arab governments (most probably in the department of *Ḥisba*), which controlled medical education and practice.[50] In Syria and Egypt we find the name of Muhadhdhab al-Dīn being authorized to certify doctors during Ayyūbid times. Ibn Abī Uṣaibi'a writes about the same period that once when he was in Cairo, the Ayyūbid ruler ordered the doctor Muhadhdhab al-Dīn to test and properly certify ophthalmologists.[51] We hear again such tests being conducted during the caliphate of al-Mustaḍī or al-Muhtadi by Ibn al-Tilmīdh.[52]

It appears that the standards of medical education, and consequently of practice as well, deteriorated after it became part of the *madrasa* education and was disassociated from hospitals. In Turkey where hospital-based education continued—whether connected with *madrasas* or not we do not know—standards remained relatively high. As state-founded or state-funded Islamic educational institutions multiplied, orthodox religious disciplines of theology and law became the center of intellectual life. In the later medieval centuries, these disciplines themselves stagnated and along with these stagnated all the scientific disciplines including medicine. The stagnation of religious disciplines was self-imposed and resulted from their own inner life. Their stagnation had naturally a deleterious effect on other sciences as well. Philosophy was particularly the bête noire of the orthodoxy. It is obvious that when philosophy and science declined this rebounded on the theological disciplines themselves which must starve due to a lack of challenge. The rigidity and lack of creativity in the fields of Islamic theology and law are the most striking features of the later medieval centuries of Islam, which have undermined the respect of the modern educated Muslim for traditional Islam, an alienation which various attempts at educational reform now seek to remedy. On the other hand, in the modern West, positive sciences and medicine gradually cut themselves loose from religious disciplines but their secularization was achieved at the high price of depriving them of a spiritual foundation.

Since the system of examinations and certification was loosely applied and in many places did not exist at all, a new type of medical literature came into being generally known as *Miḥnat al-Ṭabīb* (How to Test a Doctor). This literature was produced so that laypeople could judge for themselves whether a given person was a genuine physician or a quack. The highly independent-minded but equally hypercritical ʿAbd al-Laṭīf al-Baghdādī (d. 1231) passes, in his tractates, some sweeping judgments on those whom he regards as "the quacks of our time." On the question of testing a physician for one's own satisfaction, Galen's works on the subject served as models. Works of this genre were also used by the *muḥtasibs* for the purpose of judging the professional worth of a doctor. One such work, written about the third quarter of the thirteenth century by a certain ʿAbd al-ʿAzīz the Physician, has been described by Ḥakīm Nayyir Wāsiṭī in his Urdu commentary on E. G. Browne's *Arabian Medicine*.[53] In the introduction to the work titled *How the Wise Can Test All Physicians* (*Imtiḥān al-Alibbāʾ li-Kāffat al-Aṭibbāʾ*), the author tells us that this profession had deteriorated "because there was no check upon it" and therefore all sorts of pretenders had been exploiting it; thus "a point had been reached where barbers had started practicing ophthalmology, and surgeons and ophthalmologists had embarked on practicing internal medicine." Each of the work's ten chapters contains twenty questions and their answers, based on authentic medical works. Three chapters are about surgery, ophthalmology, and bone setting. Several questions from the chapter on the pulse pertain to the effect of feelings of pleasure and love upon the pulse's rhythm and strength, of the effect of music, why the pulse "hardens" in certain forms of dropsy, and so on. The work was so much appreciated that the Mogul emperor Akbar obtained the original copy of it. It was finally published in Delhi in 1900 by Ḥakīm Badr al-Dīn Khan with an introduction and Urdu translation.

Similarly, there existed a system of examining pharmacists. During the Abbasid period, the general al-Afshīn (put to death in 840 on suspicion of resurrecting ancient Iranian ideas and feelings against Islam) ordered Dhakarīyā ibn al-Ṭaifūrī to scrutinize pharmacists. As a result of this measure, several pharmacists had to close their businesses. Works were written on pharmacy to guide the work of pharmacists but also to facilitate examination of pharmaceutical practice. Shāpūr ibn Sahl wrote such a work on compound medicines, *al-Qarābādhīn al-A'ẓam*. Again, in connection with such exams, we hear of laxity, and the historian of medicine al-Qifṭī indicates sometimes bribery was also resorted to.[54]

SPIRITUAL MEDICINE

Spiritual medicine can be used to mean two different things, although both are allied and sometimes confused. One refers to the belief in a spiritual or ethical or psychological cure for diseases that may be physical or spiritual (or psychic). Thus, a physical illness may be cured, for example, by recitation of the Qur'an or other prayers. This belief was recognized to an extent by most medical men of Islam even in the scientific tradition of medicine. The other is the belief that illness, particularly mental illness or madness, is caused by supernatural spiritual forces. In Hellenism possession by the demons or evil spirits was a widespread belief; Christian priests claimed to cure such illness. Such beliefs were common in the Middle East, India, and probably all over the world, not necessarily exclusively but primarily in folkloric medicine.

The Islamic doctrine that all mental illnesses were caused by an imbalance of the four humors, however, ultimately emanating from Galen, ran counter to the supernatural causation of mental illness. This Galenic tradition became an essential component in the Islamic medical tradition, which also rejected ideas of demonic possession. This is common to the Islamic medical tradition and the orthodox Islamic creedal tradition. At the popular level, however, as we shall see presently, belief in possession by spirits and exorcism continued. It is interesting to note that the Prophet Muhammad was once approached by some of his tribesmen who, vexed at his persistent religious stance, suggested that he was possessed by some spirit (called *jin*) and that they could have him cured by some exorcist.[55] This suggestion of madness was strenuously and repeatedly rejected by the Qur'an, however, and hence in orthodox Islam there grew up no tradition of the "holy fool" comparable to the one that existed in early Christianity.

Despite the Galenic tradition, however, the psychic causation of illness, particularly psychic illness, was recognized by Muslims who were, unlike Galen, interactionists. Michael W. Dols writes that despite the predominance of the dogmatic tradition in Islamic medicine,

> the psychic causation subsisted in the textbooks, and various forms of psychotherapy were evidently practiced. Although many of the therapies can be found in the works of late antique authors, the use of shock or shame-therapy, particularly, by Islamic doctors seems to have been original. Thus, it appears that some Muslim physicians drew upon their own experiences and often adopted a holistic approach to medicine. The best representative of this minority view is the mid-eleventh century doctor Sa'īd ibn Bakhtīshū', who argued persuasively in one of his treatises for the psychic causation of illness, epitomized in his view by passionate love alongside the somatic. At the beginning of the fourth chapter of his work, Ibn Bakhtīshū' counters the neglect of the psychic element in illness by the ordinary doctor. "Who has not entered the *bīmāristāns* and has not seen how the staff treats the sick—pacifying the nerves of some and busying the minds of others, diverting their anxieties and entertaining them with song and with other things, exciting some of them by abuse and scorn and stirring their souls."[56]

In view of the fact that most great doctors in Islam were interactionists, it is not quite correct to call them a minority, as Dols does. A man like Ibn Sīnā who was a Galenist and belonged to the so-called Dogmatic (as opposed to the purely empirical) tradition, and who was the model for most doctors, himself is credited with psychic cures. A famous Persian work titled *The Four Essays* (*Chahār Maqāla*), written about 1155 C.E. for the ruler of Samarqand by his court-poet Niẓāmī-Ye 'Arūẕī, discusses administrators, astronomers (astrologers), poets, and physicians. Each chapter gives definitions of an ideal person in each category followed by ten illustrative anecdotes. In the chapter on physicians, a story is related about Ibn Sīnā's treatment of a prince. The young man suffered from some mental derangement, left off eating food, and thought he was a cow and that he must be slaughtered and eaten like a cow. When no treatment proved successful, Ibn Sīnā was asked to take over the desperate case. Ibn Sīnā sent word that he would be arriving on a certain day and directed that the youth be told he was coming to slaughter him and that a sharp knife be made ready. Upon his arrival, Ibn Sīnā ordered that the patient be bound hand and foot like a cow prepared to be slaughtered. The physician took the knife in his right hand and with the left hand felt the body of the patient in various places. He then stood up exclaiming, "This cow is too emaciated to be slaughtered; its flesh will be too unhealthy to be eaten. You must fatten it first and only then can I slaughter it." Thenceforward, the young prince began to eat food, and when he put on enough weight, his mental ailment was cured. A similar story has been narrated by Ibn Abī Uṣaibiʻa about the treatment by Jibrā'īl ibn Bakhtīshūʻ of a beloved slave-girl of the caliph Hārūn al-Rashīd through shock-treatment.[57]

Part of spiritual medicine in Islam, as was the case with the Greek tradition, is devoted to ethical well-being, but from a practical point of view. Thus Abū Bakr al-Rāzī wrote two works on this aspect of curing. One of these, *al-Ṭibb al-Rūḥānī* (Spiritual Medicine) has been translated into English as *The Spiritual Physick of Rhazes.*[58] In this work, al-Rāzī describes in detail the moral diseases and discusses with acute perception how these affect human behavior. The therapeutic method he recommends is that persons with such ailments, after being made aware of them, should cultivate the services of a critic-friend who should be both objective in analyzing his conduct but at the same time deeply sympathetic to him.

Another very interesting work of al-Rāzī is *al-Sīra al-Falsafiya* (The Conduct of a Philosopher), written as a defense of his personal conduct, which had been attacked by some of his opponents as unbecoming of a man of such wisdom as al-Rāzī claimed to have.[59] Al-Rāzī's unnamed attackers (probably Ismāʻīlī missionaries, since they had waged controversies with him on his alleged denial of prophethood and of all those who had spoken in God's name as his elected missionaries) had alleged that while he claimed to be a follower of Socrates in his life, he in fact enjoyed life and its good things. The essence of al-Rāzī's reply is that both excessive indulgence and excessive abstemiousness are bad, that there is a range between these two which is healthy, and that although Socrates had been abstemious in his early life, he had modified his asceticism in his later life—for example, he married and took interest in social affairs and even participated in national wars. Al-Rāzī maintains that indulgence in that pleasure is bad which, if enjoyed would bring greater harm or pain to others or to the perpetrator himself than the pain he would suffer if he were to desist from such indulgence. It would be clearly a utilitarian definition but for the fact that al-Rāzī takes into account belief in the hereafter as well. He further tells us that many people deny themselves even lawful pleasures as a kind of training in self-control so that they can control themselves when an extraordinary tempting situation of wrong pleasure presents itself. This is healthy morality unlike that of "Christian monks and many Muslim Sufis who are abstemious for the sake of abstemiousness."[60] Since lawful pleasures have a range, one cannot expect an economically high-born person to conform to a life-style of a person of modest means, although beyond a point indulgence does become wrong.

Al Rāzī claims that his entire life falls within this range of lawful pleasures, although, of course, "I cannot claim to come up to the rank of Socrates." He says he has attended rulers' courts but only as a professional medical man and has never sought to acquire political power; he has never aimed at amassing wealth and indulged in conspicuous consumption—in fact, al-Rāzi advises against "working hard in order to earn wealth simply to raise one's standard of living disproportionately." He tells us that those who know him can testify to the fact that he has always been moderate in his eating, drinking, clothing, riding, and so on. On the other hand, he has always been fond of acquiring knowledge from both books and men and has always made special efforts to do so. As for writing, "I have written in one year more than twenty thousand leaves and worked day and night for fifteen years on my book, *The Comprehensive in Medicine* (in Latin, *Continens*), until my eyesight has been badly weakened and the muscles of my hand can no longer work." Al-Rāzī adds, "Even if I were to admit, in a concessional mood, that I have been somewhat lax on the practical side, what will my opponents say about my intellectual and academic performance?"[61]

Part of what we have narrated here belongs more properly to Chapter 5 on ethics; nevertheless, al-Rāzī's statements provide us with a concrete view of the health of the mind and how to achieve and maintain it. In fact, in the view of Muslim doctors and philosophers (and in Islam, following the Greek tradition, the two have been intimately connected—the term *ḥikma*, originally meaning "wisdom," describes both philosophy and medicine, and *ḥakīm*, plural *ḥukamā'*, means both doctors and philosophers), ethical health is par excellence mental health just as is true of their opposites.

Before we turn to the question of spiritual cures, it needs to be pointed out that the presupposition of such treatments is that the constitution of the universe is basically spiritual and moral and that therefore the material existence is palpably under the impact of this spiritual reality. The Qur'an supports this position, for it continually asserts that the basic causes of the rise and decline of civilizations are moral in nature.[62] The philosopher-doctor Ibn Sīnā asserted the same in stating that by its very nature the material "obeys" the spiritual. But this outlook on life became the hallmark of Sufism. The famous Sufi Niẓām al-Dīn of Delhi (d.1325) is recorded to have told of a party of Muslim merchants from Lahore who took their cloth merchandise to Gujarat in order to market it there to Hindu merchants. For every piece of cloth, they first stated the price to be twice what it really was. Afterward they sold the cloth at its real price, thus giving the impression that they were giving a big bargain to their customers. One of the Gujarati merchants, shocked at these tactics, asked the visiting traders where they came from. Upon hearing they came from Lahore, he asked, "Is this a common trading practice in Lahore?" When the Lahorites replied "yes," he asked whether Lahore was still there. "Yes," they replied, upon which the Gujarati exclaimed, "A city in which this kind of trading ethics goes on cannot survive for long." Niẓām al-Dīn comments that while these merchants were on their way to Lahore, the Mongols attacked the city and sacked it.[63]

This anecdote about the destruction of Lahore underlines the principle of the influence of the spiritual over the material. Belief in the operation of spiritual forces explains the abundance of the use of prayers and amulets in the Muslim world particularly in the Sufi circles and the masses at large who were under the powerful influence of Sufi shaikhs. The Mogul emperor Jehāngīr once suffered from some illness which his doctors were unable to cure. Frustrated, he repaired to the tomb of the Saint Mu'īn al-Dīn Chishtī at Ajmer and was cured. Ever since then he wore ear-rings in the name of the saint as a token of being his follower.[64]

Volumes of spiritual prescriptions for cures exist. Most of these consist of prayers. As mentioned above, the Prophet was reluctant to permit amulets—in fact, he first prohibited them and reluctantly allowed them only when some followers insisted, but he did stipulate that no amulet contain any suggestion of ascribing to any creature supranatural powers or the sharing of divinity with God. As a result, most prayers and amulets contain verses from the Qur'an, to which high curative powers were ascribed—for the Qur'an, as said before, calls itself a "cure" although it has in mind the quality of creating and sustaining faith, not necessarily physical cure. Very frequently, the recommendation is made that the patient shall write down certain Qur'anic verses on a piece of paper or on a glass and after soaking these writings in water, drink the water. Sometimes timings are also prescribed, for example, "before sunrise."

In the famous bibliographical work of the seventeenth-century Ottoman writer Ḥājjī Khalīfa titled *Kashf al-Ẓunūn*, three works are mentioned, each titled *Khawāṣṣ al-Qur'an* (Miraculous Properties of the Qur'an.) The earliest of these belongs to the ninth-century writer al-Ḥakīm al-Tamīmī.[65] In this work, the "miraculous properties" of practically each passage of the Qur'an are discussed including their curative properties for various diseases. Indeed, each chapter of the Qur'an is represented as having different benefits when read in a different manner. About chapter 38 (which deals mainly with three topics: the penalties for *ẓihār*, a form of willful repudiation of a wife by a husband; the prohibition of conspiratorial cliquing; and the teaching of respect for Muhammad), for example, it is said that when recited on a sleeping person it cures breathing problems; when written down and read during a patient's waking hours, it cures illness. A person who continuously recites it will be immune from all troubles at night, while a person reciting the chapter over a hidden treasure insures that it will remain safe until he reclaims it. Indeed, certain passages of the Qur'an, when constantly recited, facilitate a proper understanding of the meaning of the Qur'an itself.

Curative powers are also attributed to the Sufi shaikhs. These powers are seen in Ewing's 1980 account of visits made to a Sufi (also called *pīr*, Persian equivalent of the Arabic *shaikh*) by his followers:

> Because of [the omniscient] power of the Pīr, it is not considered necessary for the Pīr to engage in a long interaction with his follower. The visitor gives a brief account of the specific problem that is troubling him. These accounts usually are as formulaic as the Pīr's responses are. In the course of observation of one Pīr, I heard many people narrate their complaints. These complaints included such things as sickness, infertility, problems with one's job, and fear of failure in an exam. As a few perceptive followers pointed out, however, the specific complaint which the visitor recounts is often not the "real trouble." The actual problem may be a vague anxiety or it may be something that the person is too embarrassed to talk about. Such misrepresentation is specially common, when, as is often the case, a spouse or other relative has accompanied the troubled person. In one instance which I witnessed, two sisters-in-law visited

> a Pīr. One complained of fatigue and the other asked for an amulet for her child. In this particular case it was a quiet day, and one of the women was able to linger behind until she was alone with the Pīr (and me). She then revealed that her sister-in-law was sleeping with her husband. The Pīr gave her advice on how to be more appealing to her husband. Candidness in this situation was, at least in my observation, unusual. A visitor is rarely alone with the Pīr. The standardization of complaints may also be a product of the limits of the vocabulary of distress. This distress may be, in our (Western) way of looking at it, either "physical" or "mental": the two cannot be separated phenomenologically. The patient merely names the part of the body or the area of his life where he perceives his distress to be concentrated. Because of their belief in the omniscience of the Pīr, however, followers do not consider it to be necessary to represent their problems accurately. The Pīr will penetrate to the heart of the problem regardless of what is said.[66]

Ewing goes on to explain the principle behind the cures of exorcism, which are basically no different from the ordinary cures by amulets and prayers, except that exorcism is much more ritualized: namely, that the pīr exercises the supranatural powers necessary to exorcise the spirit(s) possessing the patient.

·5·

Medical Ethics

Medical ethics in Islam is part of a special branch of literature known as *adab*. *Adab* in the literature of Ḥadīth and early post-Islamic literature means "proper manners," "good etiquette," "correct procedure," but it also comes to mean ethics. There are works on the ethics of judges, of government secretaries, of government ministers, of companions, of teachers and students. There are also works on medical ethics. These seek to inculcate good practical morals accompanied by "professional ethics" in respective fields. Practical piety and high character are emphasized in connection with all professions. For example, al-Ghazālī says that although a jurist does not have to be a pious person in order to be a competent jurist, because a jurist's work is essentially intellectual, nevertheless piety and good character aid in the general acceptance of the jurist's views and bad character would detract from their value.[1]

General piety and sincerity in the character of a physician were emphasized by Greek medical men, who were regarded as custodians of both body and soul. However, this is true of all developed cultures of the ancient and medieval world. In ancient Egypt, Iran, and India, medicine was either a part of religion or very closely related to it. On medical ethics in Islam, as on ethics in general, there have been two direct influences: the Greek and the Iranian, the former being the more textual and concretely visible. The Hippocratic oath for physicians is patently to be found in several works. However, the ideas of balance, the mean, and proportionality are not exclusively Greek, they are conspicuously present in the Qur'an and the Persian tradition as well.[2]

Whether a doctor should charge a fee and if so, how much, was an often debated question in Islam. It seems to have been part of the much larger question whether a teacher should accept remuneration, particularly a teacher of religion.[3] Even today, some defend the thesis that it is unlawful to charge fees for teaching the Qur'an and for imparting religious knowledge.[4] Al-Rāzī as we have seen, insisted in self-defense that he had never treated people for the object of amassing wealth. Yet Jibrā'īl ibn Bakhtīshū', Hārūn al-Rashīd's physician, earned almost 5 million dirhams annually for his work at the caliphal court, although people who hired him —caliphs and nobles—could well afford to pay these large sums. According to Prophetic Ḥadīth, it is lawful to pay a physician for his medical services. Al-Dhahabī narrates that once when a traveling party of Muslims reached a certain tribe, the latter withheld hospitality from them. But in the meantime, someone from the tribe was bitten by a snake, and the travelers were asked if they could cure him. According to one version, this was done by reciting the opening chapter of the Qur'an, while the other version says that the tribesmen asked for a medicine. In any case, the afflicted person was cured, and the tribe paid a number of goats—according to one report, a hundred goats—a transaction reportedly approved by the Prophet, who also asked for a share. Upon this tradition is based the legality of charging a fee for medical treatment.[5] Many, however, do not approve of making a living out of treating the sick. A certain physician 'Abd al-Wadūd ibn 'Abd al-Mālik wrote a treatise (still unpublished) titled "In Denunciation of One Who Makes His Living by the Art of Treating the Sick."[6]

Among the earliest and most comprehensive statements on medical ethics is *Adab al-Ṭabīb* (The Ethics of the Physician), the work of Isḥāq ibn 'Alī al-Ruhāvī, who probably lived in the second half of the ninth century.[7] Al Ruhāvī insists that it is a physician's duty to interrelate the spiritual and bodily health: "The philosophers can only improve the soul, but the virtuous physician can improve both body and soul. The physician deserves the claim that he is imitating the acts of God the Exalted as much as he can." He says on the authority of Galen that Hippocrates had advocated in *On Belief* that a would-be medical student undergo an examination in both body and soul. Before the physician could treat the patient as a whole, he or she should be or should become a whole. A doctor's daily routine should be as follows: "He should wash his mouth, clean and polish his teeth. Then it is necessary to examine the order of his bodily organs. . . . His clothes should be useful and attractive. Following all this is prayer. Then he should read the book of his religion, then books of the ancients on medicine."[8] Then comes his professional routine—the house visits and the office practice.

The physician should frequent the assemblages of the virtuous and the learned. Further, he should not buy property or engage in trade, since this would prevent him from the pursuit of science. On doctors' fees, al-Ruhāvī states that a doctor should earn enough to alleviate the necessity of doing other work, to raise children and educate them in the art of medicine, and also to afford marriage and a comfortable family life. That the medical career was thought of as a vocation rather than as a profession generally characterizes both the theory and practice of medicine in Islam. Thus al-Ruhāvī states that the rich must pay the physician generously so that he can look after the medical needs of the poor without charge. If the rich do not do so, physicians would be forced to give up their medical work and follow some other profession, and rich and poor alike would suffer.[9] As hinted above, this practice has been largely followed by medieval physicians in Islam through their clinics (apart from free hospitals).

The doctor Isḥāq the Isrā'īlite (date of death given differently as 932 or 955, the latter being more popular with recent writers) is credited with a work containing fifty aphorisms; the work seems to be lost in the Arabic original but is preserved in a Hebrew translation. Aphorism 18 states: "Visiting and healing the poor and needy patients is your special duty because a more meritorious work you cannot perform."[10] Isḥāq provides another example of the intimate relationship between religion and medicine from the outset in the history of Islam. This same spirit patently underlies the phenomenon of Prophetic Medicine. One is led to venture a bold suggestion. Medical authorities were claiming religion for medicine; could the authors of the Prophetic Medicine be reacting by claiming medicine for religion? This would be not only congruent with but would, indeed, corroborate the thesis that the Prophetic Medicine literature aimed at setting high religious value on medicine in order to claim it for religion.

Be that as it may, Abū Bakr al-Rāzī is of the view that both patient and physician have to observe an ethical discipline.[11] He advises all patients that they should strictly follow their physicians' orders, that they should respect their physicians, and indeed should consider them better than their best friends. Patients should have direct contact with their doctors and not keep any secret from them concerning an ailment. Indeed, it is better for people to be in touch with a doctor who can advise them how to stay healthy before they actually need treatment. That prevention is better than cure is a principle subscribed to by all doctors, including Muslim doctors; but al-Rāzī insisted that people consult doctors on how best to preserve health.

Al-Rāzī also has a good deal of advice and requirements for physicians. Among these is that a physician should be a cultured person. Al-Rāzī also insists that the physician gain the trust of the patient and cultivate professional confidence. Al-Rāzī himself is acknowledged by all Muslim historians of medicine as being not only patient with but positively kind and merciful toward all his patients. Further, a physician must try to be self-reliant and original because inherited knowledge gained from books alone is far from sufficient.[12] Al-Rāzī had so many students and patients, we are told, that when a patient first came to his hospital, he/she was seen by his students' students; if they failed, the patient was seen by his direct students, and only when they failed was the patient brought to the master. But when the patient did come to al-Rāzī, he left no stone unturned in diagnosis and treatment. A number of stories are related in this connection. One patient, for example, suffered from an irregular fever along with frequent urination. After a prolonged examination, al-Rāzī determined that the man had a kidney infection, adding that if the patient had told him sooner that he felt pressure in the back when he stood, he might have diagnosed it earlier.[13]

Al-Rāzī also advises that a physician must never lose patience with a patient whether poor or rich. The physician must lead a balanced and moderate life and not waste time and energy indulging in pleasures and amusements. Time should be given generously to a patient; the physician should listen more and talk less. Finally, al-Rāzī advises that a physician must never be discouraged but take pride in his profession because all religions are unanimous in honoring physicians: the very term for a physician—*ḥakīm*, which means full of knowledge and wisdom in Arabic—is one of the names of God in Islam. Neither a common man nor a king can afford to do without a physician; hence the latter must make patients happy.[14]

In *The Four Essays* (mentioned in Chapter 4 in the section on spiritual medicine), Niẓāmī discusses the ethics of the doctor:

> A physician should be of kindly disposition, characterized by rational thought and possessed of excellent intuitive power. Intuition is a movement of the mind whereby it hits at correct opinion, that is, a quick passage from the known to the unknown. . . . Now, a physician who does not recognize the nobility of man cannot have a kindly disposition, one who is not well-versed in logic cannot have rational thinking, and one who does not have God's support [a divine gift] cannot possess an excellent intuitive power. Without the gift of intuitive power, a person cannot know the correct cause [of an ailment], because his guide has to be the pulse. Now pulse has the motions of contraction and expansion and the interval that is between the two. . . .

The mental-moral-spiritual aspect of a physician's work, then, is highly valued. Among the ten anecdotes that follow, several deal with the psychological or spiritual treatment of physical maladies. One interesting anecdote is from Ibn Sīnā. Ibn Sīnā had heard the story of a physician who was very close to a Sāmānid ruler (Sāmānid Turks ruled northeastern Iran and the Syr-Oxus basin in Central Asia through the tenth century), so close that he was freely admitted to the *ḥaram* quarters of the king, where he personally treated the royal household. Once the king asked him to dine with him while both were in the *ḥaram* quarters. During the dinner a servant brought a dish and bent to put it on the carpet. When she tried to stand up straight, she was unable to, and despite her repeated efforts she could not: she apparently had a severe attack of lumbago. No medical treatment was available, but the king asked the physician to do what he could. The physician asked that her scarf be removed and her hair exposed (which was immodest for a woman to do among men). When she still did not respond, the physician asked that her trouser be pulled off. When she saw her trouser being pulled off, she stood up straight and got away through the shock of shame. Her lumbago was cured.[15] Ibn Sīnā quotes this to prove that certain psychological-spiritual phenomena can overcome physical disabilities, showing the influence of the mind on the body.

In another anecdote Niẓāmī-Ye 'Arūẕī tells of a spectacular case of spiritual healing that he heard in the year 512 A.H. (1118 C.E.) in the druggists' market in Nīshāpūr in Iran. Khawāja Abū Bakr, a dealer in powdered medicines, told him,

> In 502 A.H. (1108 C.E.) I was asked to treat one of the prominent citizens of Nīshāpūr who was suffering from severe colic. I examined him and treated him, but he did not respond. Three days passed and no medicine worked. On the third day, I returned from the evening prayers without any hope of the patient's recovery and, in fact, expected that he would pass away during the night. I slept but was quite worried. In the morning I got up convinced that he must have died. I went upstairs and looked toward the patient's home but, after listening well, could hear no voices [of mourners] that might indicate his death. I recited the Opening *Sura* of the Qur'an and blew with my breath in that direction, and prayed, "O my Lord, my God, my Master! You have said in your firm, true, and indubitable Book [the Qur'an], "We send down the Qur'an as a restorer of health and as mercy for the believers [17, 82]." As I recited this prayer, I felt sad at the thought that he was a young man, both prosperous and generous, but he was ending his life this way. Then I performed ablutions, stood on the prayer rug, and began praying. Someone called out from the yard. I looked and he gave me the good news, "Smile!" I asked, "What is the matter?" He said, "Your patient is well." I was convinced that this was due to the recitation of the Opening *Sura* of the Qur'an. After this, I repeated it on several occasions and it was effective.[16]

In Islam, ethics and spiritual medicine belong to the same complex of ideas, and it is not possible to separate them completely, as seen in the works of al-Rāzī. His *Conduct of a Philosopher* lays out an ideal of spiritual health and gives a defense of his own way of life. In *Spiritual Medicine* he considers the problem of how to treat one's own ethical ailments. Both works corroborate reports given by Muslim historians of medicine that al-Rāzī was particularly concerned with ethical questions connected to medicine. Particularly since medicine and philosophy were closely allied to Islam, as they were in Greek tradition, ethical questions assume a double importance. First is the ethical responsibility of the physician toward the patient, which has two dimensions in Islam. One is the relationship of the doctor to the patient: the kindness, patience, concern, and professional confidence owed to the patient. The other is the strong belief that unless physicians are themselves good and ethical people, their treatment will not be effective—quite apart from the consideration that an unethical physician will not have a good reputation and will not, therefore, be successful. Second, in Islam ethical health is part of general health, and unless a person has good, positive, and balanced morals, he or she cannot maintain general health either. Thus both moral health and physical health become, from this perspective, a directly medical concern. This is the subject of al-Rāzī's *Spiritual Medicine.* Al-Rāzī introduces his work by saying, "In the court of the amir [the ruler] Manṣūr ibn Isḥāq, there ensued a discussion on reforming morals. He asked me to write him a monograph on the subject and call it *Spiritual Medicine* so that it would be a companion volume to my work *Al-Manṣūrī* [so-called because it was dedicated to this ruler], the object of which was physical medicine. And he asked that it be equal to this other work in being of general benefit and in comprehending both soul and body."[17]

The work opens with a statement on the importance of reason, whereby man is distinguished from animals, and stresses the necessity for man to make reason his guide. In the body of the book, uninformed and uneducated instincts and desires (*hawā'*, plural *ahwā'*) are opposed to reason, and certain measures are suggested for either overcoming such desires or taming them and rechanneling them: "The greatest and noblest principle and the one most helpful in achieving the object of this book is [either] to uproot such desires and to oppose what natural lusts invite us to in most cases [or] to train the soul toward them gradually. For this is the primary excellence of man over animals, that is, the capacity to form a will [from a wish] and execute an act after proper deliberation."[18] As noted above, the author also recommends that in order to assess and remedy one's moral faults, one must have recourse to a sympathetic and concerned friend who watches one's conduct and gives constructive advice.

Al-Rāzī enumerates fourteen moral ailments, the first of which is love. In the medical writings of Islam, love plays a strikingly prominent role as a mental-moral malady; author after author talks about it, and stories and anecdotes about lovers abound in literature. There are stories (probably apocryphal) about how Ibn Sīnā diagnosed lovers' maladies (particularly those of princes who were averse to telling anyone that they were madly in love with someone) by continuously feeling the patient's pulse and monitoring its rhythm and also watching his facial expression while questioning him about localities where his beloved may possibly be living, mentioning various females' names living there, or having someone describe the geography of the various quarters.[19] In any case, al-Rāzī tells us that people with high goals and ambitions in life do not normally fall in love, and when they do, they get out of it quickly because it humiliates and dishonors those afflicted with it and that only coarse and unrefined people like the Bedouin fall prey to this malady. The remedy al-Rāzī suggests is to see one's beloved less often until one weans oneself completely; remembering that finally all lovers must be parted by death will also help. To allow physical love to develop into a deeper, psychological attachment only makes things worse, and the only thing that can help is to cultivate some other valuable goal and interest in life.[20]

Al-Rāzī suggests that moral ailments be treated on the basis of a distinction he makes between those who believe in an afterlife and those who do not. Thus, on the question of love, those who do not believe in an afterlife should consider that this worldly love is someday going to be cut off by death, and hence one should strive for something that has real value, while those who believe in an afterlife know that the real object of love to be pursued is that which will earn a richer life for the mind after death. This distinction is made in more fundamental terms in chapter 2, which concerns the problem of lower desires and how to uproot them, "in accordance with the theory of Plato." There he states that the first and most basic step in moral training is what the child receives at a young age—something which domesticated animals are also capable of but which a normal child is much better at. A more rational basis of morals after such training is the awareness that when one keeps indulging in a certain pleasure—for example, sex or alcohol, it ceases to be pleasurable, and yet one cannot discard it or does not want to do so because it has become a settled habit and addiction whose absence gives pain but whose presence does not yield enjoyment. It is like a trap into which an animal falls, attracted first by some food that has been put there to entice it but later finding it to be poison:

> This kind of morality is upheld and advocated by those philosophers who do not hold that the soul is self-subsisting substance and that it is destroyed with the destruction of the body. However, as for those who believe that the soul is an independent being and self-subsisting substance [that is, apart from the body] and that it is not destroyed with physical death, they rise farther in controlling their natural, uninformed instincts and desires, and several condemn and castigate those who submit to their desires and consider them just like animals.[21]

This principle is employed perhaps most spectacularly in al-Rāzī's discussion of how to combat the fear of death. He tells us that this particular ailment can be cured, if at all, by convincing the patient that the condition in which the soul can be after death is much superior to its condition in this life. For those who disbelieve in an afterlife, al-Rāzī puts forward two arguments. One, that it can be demonstrated that pleasure is the avoidance of or escape from pain, which is available only after death, and second, that when one knows something to be inevitable, it is useless to grieve about it and much better to turn one's attention away from it to something uesful. Both these answers involve conquest of instincts by the power of reason, says al-Rāzī, adding that unthinking animals appear to be better than man in this respect for they have no knowledge of the inevitability of death—not that animals are superior to man but that, from this point of view, they are more fortunately placed. For the person who does not believe in life after death, the best alternative is to turn one's mind away from death, for a person who thinks of death, without believing in the hereafter, dies every time he thinks of it.[22]

But the first argument is more involved than it appears at first, for the proposition that the condition after death is better than that of life is controversial. Al-Rāzī contends that because there is no pain after death, according to the belief of these people the state after death is better than that of life, where there is much pain. The opponent then urges that although there is much pain in life, there is also much pleasure, which disappears with death. Al-Rāzī replies that because *there is no need or longing for pleasure after death,* lack of pleasure does not harm. There would be pain if there were need or longing for pleasure (that is, desire) which was thwarted. The opponent objects to the use of terms like pleasure, pain, longing, and desire to describe the state after death because they are inappropriate, to which al-Rāzī replies that his use of these terms for the state after death is meant not literally, but only as an analogy. This is because his opponents analogize death with life and are then sad because there would be no pleasure after death. It is on the basis of this instinctive, irrational belief of theirs—

namely, that life after death, in which they do not believe, ought to be analogous to life here—that reason passes its judgment that there will be no pain there. If their thinking were based on reason rather than on uninformed impulse, they would accept this truth even though the passions of the soul do not want to accept it.

As for those holding the view that there is an afterlife after death, they have no reason to fear death either, for if they really believe in an afterlife, they will have lived lives of virtue and excellence and done their best to carry out the obligations laid down by their true religion, which has promised success, peace, and eternal bliss in the hereafter. But should some entertain doubt about the truth of religion and be unable to establish its truth for themselves, then they cannot do better than search and investigate this matter to the best of their ability. If they make proper effort to find the truth, they will be unlikely to miss it. However, should they miss the truth, which, as we said, is improbable, then God will surely forgive, for God never burdens anyone beyond his or her capacity (Qur'an 2, 283, 286; 6, 152; 7, 42)—indeed, his demands are much less than human capacities.[23]

Al-Rāzī's work on spiritual-moral medicine was criticized by the well-known Ismā'īlī intellectual and missionary Ḥamīd al-Dīn al-Kirmānī (d. 1020). The essence of this refutation is that al-Rāzī counts certain ailments as mental-moral while they are, in fact, physical, for example, excessive indulgence in sex. But the most basic and persistent criticism al-Kirmānī makes against al-Rāzī is that al-Rāzī believes the morally ailing can cure themselves by their own effort. We have already seen al-Rāzī saying that a person in need of moral improvement should get the help of a friend who is both sympathetic and critical. Al-Kirmānī, however, demands much more than that, namely, that every person must believe in and submit to the heavenly message which is truly enshrined in the Ismā'īlī esoteric doctrine and that no cure exists besides that, certainly not reliance on one's own intelligence. There is little doubt that here al-Kirmānī is subtly playing his role as an Ismā'īlī missionary.[24]

Throughout Islamic history, there have been reports that al-Rāzī did not believe in any religion and denied the possibility of prophethood and revelation. These reports about his irreligion have found their way into Muslim works of medical history as well. However, evidence from his works goes against such reports. We have quoted him above as saying that a person who carries out the imperatives of his or her *true* religious law has nothing to fear. Also, in *Spiritual Medicine* he says that there are some litterateurs and poets who even attribute the sickness of love to prophets.[25] Al-Rāzī, who was involved in numerous controversies with some of his contemporaries, had particularly incensed the Ismāʿīlīs because of his debate with Abū Ḥātim al-Rāzī (d.934), the greatest representative Ismāʿīlī intellectual and missionary of his day (who came from the same town as al-Rāzī). The only report of this debate we have is from the Ismāʿīlī missionary, wherein Abū Bakr al-Rāzī is represented as denying the possibility of prophethood and revelation on the basis of the universality of divine guidance. But the statements quoted herein appear to refute Ismāʿīlī allegations. It may well be true that, confronted with Ismāʿīlī doctrines of esoteric teaching (*al-Taʿlīm*) and electionism, al-Rāzī denied the possibility of God's arbitrary choice of his messengers.

HUMAN DIGNITY

At the end of the story of Abel and Cain, the Qur'an says, "For this reason we decreed it for the children of Israel that whosoever kills a [single] human for other than murder or other than the corruption of the earth [war], it is as though he has killed all humankind and whosoever has saved one human, it is as though he has saved all humankind. And after [this decree] messengers from us have come to them [with this message], yet many of them continue to commit excesses on the earth" (5,32). While giving permission to those Muslims who had been forced to leave Mecca because of religious persecution to fight in order to get back their homes and lands—the first pronouncement on *jihād*—the Qur'an gives the rationale behind the *jihād*: "But for the fact that God repels some people [who commit excesses] through others, cloisters, churches, places of worship, and mosques wherein God's name is frequently remembered would be destroyed, and God shall help those who help him—God is powerful and mighty" (22, 40).

These passages show that human life is irreplaceable and that each human indeed is unique, and further that freedom of religion and conscience is the foundation stone of human life, because the basis of the permission for or obligation to *jihād* is persecution on grounds of belief or conscience. The concept of personal honor (*ʿirḍ*) was one of the most fundamental principles of life in pre-Islamic tribal Arabia. Around this was woven a fabric of values which the pre-Islamic Arabs called "manliness" (*muruwwa*). This list of "virtues" included defense of tribal, personal, and particularly female honor (this is why among some Arabs infanticide of girls became common and was, in fact, regarded as sanctioned by their gods [Qur'an 6, 137]—for rather than bear the unbearable burden of defending woman's honor in frequent wars, it was better to kill the girl as soon as she was born), bravery, hospitality, keeping of promises, and vengeance (*tha'r*)—according to which it was not necessarily the killer whose life was claimed in revenge *but a person in the killer's tribe whose life was equivalent in value* (in tribal terms) *to that of the person killed.* The Qur'an tried to eliminate or weaken as much as possible the tribal honor and substitute for it the community of faith. Infanticide of girls and vengeance were prohibited by the Qur'an, but the rest of these virtues were encouraged.

It is in this background that Muslim jurists laid down their theory of five basic human rights which it was the duty of the state (that is, the caliph) to protect. The first of these rights is the protection of life, followed by protection of property, of faith, of honor, and of reason.[26] Basically, honor sustains all the rest, for threat or danger to life, property, religion, and reason (*aql*) are all threats to one's honor. In its more precise form, however, protection of honor, according to the jurists, meant "the protection of private honor [*ḥurmat al-baiḍa*] and the family so that a person is free to pursue his trade or profession." Protection of reason means that the integrity of human mental faculties must be preserved; that is based on the consideration that it is rationality that distinguishes man from the rest of creation, so that once a person's reason is lost his or her humanness is lost. We recall the endowment-document of the Nūrī hospital, mentioned in Chapter 4, which particularly stressed the treatment of mental patients because a person who suffered from loss of mind lost his or her honor completely. This is not to claim that the practice of Islam has always lived up to its ideals, and from a political perspective, it has sometimes been unfair (for example, to Hindus in India), but Islam has been generally conspicuously tolerant. We have seen in our discussion of hospitals in Chapter 4 how open-minded Muslims have been both to non-Muslim physicians and non-Muslim patients.

THE FAMILY

In this section I shall discuss the family as a social unit,[27] while questions on sexuality will be the subject of the next chapter, "Passages." The Qur'an declares sex-pairing to be a universal law operative in all things ("Everything we have created in pairs" [51, 49]), and it appears that the permission for polygamy was originally given within the context of problems encountered in the treatment of orphan girls. The Qur'an (4, 2) accuses some custodians of orphans (the abundance of orphans and widows was due to the frequent intertribal wars, some of which lasted for several generations) of misappropriating their wards' properties or otherwise exploiting them unlawfully. The Qur'an had been complaining about this for some time even before the Prophet moved from Mecca to Medina in 622 (17, 34; 6, 152). In 4, 127 the Qur'an accuses most custodians of desiring to marry girl-orphans when they came of age rather than return their properties to them. In 4, 3 the Qur'an says, "If you fear that you will not be fair to [female] orphans [with regard to their properties] then you may marry them up to four; but if you fear you will not be able to do justice [among co-wives] then marry only one or [marry] your slave-women—this is nearest to the point that you will not go astray." In 4, 129 the Qur'an tells them, "And you shall never be able to do justice among women [co-wives], no matter how much you desire." The permission for polygamy was dependent upon doing justice among co-wives together with the warning that such justice was impossible to attain.

What is remarkable about the above-quoted passages is the way the Qur'an struggled with this problem. However, as the law developed on the subject—and so far as we know, the practical attitude of the community as well from the earliest documented times—the permission for polygamy up to four wives was made unconditional.[28] The reasoning of the classical lawyers of Islam was that although the permissive clause has legal force, the fulfillment of the requirement of justice is a "recommendation" which the husband should observe, that is, this requirement had a moral, not a legal force. Legally, of course, if a wife was not fairly treated, she could always go to the court for redress or divorce, which had been provided by Islam from the very beginning.

In most Muslim countries, the law on polygamy has been changed in the present century. In Turkey and Tunisia, polygamy has been banned (in the former on a secular basis, in the latter on the Qur'anic basis); other major Muslim countries except Saudi Arabia have put severe restrictions on it, requiring prior permission of a court or a tribunal if the husband wants a second wife while the first marriage subsists. In most of these countries, such permission is granted if the first wife is invalid or barren or, in some countries, if she has not borne a male issue. The consent of the first wife is, however, required.

Classical Islamic law also permitted the marriage of minors, provided it was contracted by their parents—and no other guardian—on their behalf. The reasons for this institution were sociological. Both the boy and the girl, however, could repudiate such marriage at coming of age, provided they had not consummated the marriage. In the modern reformed law, child marriage has been banned and the minimal marriage age for each of the sexes has been fixed, usually at sixteen and eighteen for the girl and the boy respectively but in some cases, as in Tunisia, at eighteen and twenty-one respectively.

The Qur'an definitely encourages marriage and discourages celibacy, but the generally prevalent notion among Western scholarly circles that it prohibits celibacy is false. The Qur'an praises Christian monks for their saintly character (5, 82), although it accuses many of them (as well as Jewish rabbis) of "consuming unlawfully people's properties and thwarting the cause of God" (9, 34). Western scholars' impression is based on Qur'an 57, 27: "Then we followed up [the earlier prophets] with Jesus son of Mary, and we gave him the Evangel, and we put in the hearts of his followers kindness and mercy; but as for monasticism, they invented it themselves—we had not laid it down upon them, [we only asked them] to pursue God's pleasure—but [having invented it themselves], they did not observe its demand properly. We gave such of them as believed their reward, but many of them are unrighteous." This verse tells us that *organized monasticism as a way of life* is unrealistic and hence unacceptable, but it does not ban individuals from observing celibacy. In fact, there have been numerous 'Ulama and also some Sufis in the recorded history of Islam who have been celibates, although marriage has been the general rule in both groups.

Severance of marital ties has several forms in classical Islamic law. A husband could repudiate his wife by a formula known as *ṭalāq* (to set free). Simple retraction of *ṭalāq* and reconciliation were possible within three months after the husband pronounced the *ṭalāq*; after three months, *ṭalāq* became effective, but remarriage was normally possible, and this process was repeatable twice. However, a heinous form of *ṭalāq* came into being in early Islam after the Prophet's death called "triple *ṭalāq*," whereby the husband by pronouncing *ṭalāq* three times in a single sitting repudiated his wife absolutely without any chance for reconciliation or remarriage. This form of repudiation produced incalculable harm in Muslim countries, particularly in the lower strata of society where husbands often repudiated their wives in a fit of temper but then repented without any remedy being available, except that the woman be married to another man with the understanding that this marriage was temporary and that the new second husband would divorce her soon so she could be remarried to the first husband. This form of repudiation of marriage is reported to have been introduced by 'Umar I, in whose time a good deal of sexual chaos ensued in Mecca and Medina due to the large influx of women prisoners of war resulting from rapid conquests. His legislation was meant as a *penal measure*: it had been reported to him that, because of the superabundance of women, men played with them, divorcing them and then retracting their divorce in order to torture them. New legislation in Muslim countries including Saudi Arabia has done away with this kind of divorce completely and, in most countries, has vested the right of granting divorce in courts.

The wife can sue for divorce on certain grounds including cruelty, neglect, desertion, and nonpayment of household expenses (under Islamic law the husband alone has the financial responsibility for the household). Also in Islamic law, marriage is a contract, albeit a solemn one, and a woman can therefore have inserted into this contract any reasonable conditions: for example, that her husband will pay her a special allowance or that he will not marry another wife. According to a classical law, the "law of delegation" (*tafwīḍ*), a husband could abdicate his right of divorce in favor of his wife.

Shi'a law allows a form of temporary marriage called *mut'a*,[29] which was present in pre-Islamic Arabia but prohibited in Islam most probably by the second caliph 'Umar I (d. 643), although it was already strongly discouraged by the Prophet. It is prevalent among the Shi'a of Iran where, although it was passively discouraged by governments before Khomeini's, it is being greatly strengthened by the current regime. This type of marriage is like an ordinary marriage in its enactment procedure but differs from it in two cardinal respects. First, it is contracted for a named period of time—from a few hours to several years—and second, at the end of the stipulated period it stands automatically terminated without formal divorce. Shi'a lawyers differ on whether a virgin can contract a *mut'a* marriage and whether children born of such marriage can inherit. It is, however, becoming much less common among the modern educated classes.

In its inheritance laws, the Qur'an assigns to a daughter one-half the share of a son (the class of female inheritors was introduced by the Qur'an).[30] In recent modernist Muslim thought there has been some debate whether all children should not get equal shares. Those who are against such proposals contend that a girl also gets a dower (*mahr*) from her husband at marriage (which is not regarded as valid without such dower); in view of this and the fact that the financial support of the household is entirely the responsibility of the husband, it is claimed that equalizing inheritance shares will constitute not justice but injustice, that is, injustice to male children.

In general, the Qur'an speaks of the husband-wife relationship as that of "mutual love and mercy" (30, 21). It describes their support for each other by saying "they [your wives] are garments unto you and you are garments unto them" (2, 187). By the term *garment*, which occurs in the Qur'an in varying contexts, is meant something that soothes and covers up one's weaknesses. As for rights and duties, it declares (2, 228): "For them [women] there are rights [against men] that are exactly commensurate with their duties [toward them], but men are one degree higher [than women]." Elsewhere the rationale for this disparity in the socioeconomic sector is given by saying that men work and earn money and hence are more excellent. In recent debates, again, the question is being asked whether the male superiority would not disappear if women were educated and acquired the same skills and earning power as men.

There is little doubt that, through the medium of the Ḥadīth, the amalgam of cultures that entered Islam after conquests imposed its own ethos on the Qur'anic doctrine, causing major deviations from the Qur'anic norms. The Qur'an, for example, with unflinching regularity mentions men and women separately as being absolute equals in points of virtue and piety: "Those who have surrendered to God's law, of males and females, those who believe, of males and females, those who are sincere, of males and females, those who are truthful, of males and females, those who are patient, of males and females, those who fear God, of males and females, those who give in charity, of males and females, those who fast, of males and females, those who preserve their chastity, of males and females, those who remember God often, of males and females—God has prepared for them forgiveness and great reward" (33, 35). When we come to Ḥadīth, however, we are presented with a quite different picture. According to a famous and historically influential Ḥadīth, the Prophet once passed by some women and said, "O you women! You must be extra careful to be good for I have seen most of you in hell. I have not seen a creature weaker both in religion and in intelligence than you who yet overpowers the wits of a man of sound reason." "What is the weakness in our religion?" the women asked, and got the reply, "Is it not the case that when you menstruate, you are required neither to pray nor to fast?" "Yes," said the women, "but what is the weakness of our intelligence?" "Is not the evidence of one of you [in court] half that of a male's?" "Yes," the women replied.

As for the "weakness" of women in religion, the single lengthy Qur'anic verse just quoted by us is sufficient to destroy it. But the part of this Ḥadīth which speaks of the evidentiary value of female statements as being half that of men is still more interesting because it presupposes the development of the law of evidence in early Islam. The law is supposed to be based on Qur'an 2, 282, which states that in a case of borrowing and lending, the transaction should be written down and that two good, reliable male witnesses should witness it. If, however, two such males are not available, then one male and two female witnesses are required, "because should one of the females make an error [in giving evidence] the other would remind her." The Qur'an is not, of course, enacting any general law about the comparative value of male and female evidence here but talking about a specific type of transaction. Second, if this law were correct, the Qur'an would have allowed the substitution of four women for two men, yet it insisted that one male witness be present. Because the case the Qur'an is speaking of is that of a financial transaction and because most women in those days did not deal with finances or with business in general, the Qur'an thought it better to have two women instead of one—*if one had to have women*. This means, of course, that if women should get education equal to men's and also become conversant with business and finance, the law must change accordingly.

BIOETHICAL ISSUES

Problems of bioethics and genetic engineering belong to the contemporary age and in the Muslim world have not, so far as I know, yet become the subject of overt and systematic discussion. The recently founded Islamic Medical Association of North America has on its agenda problems like artificial insemination, but no publications of any discussions, if any have taken place, have so far appeared. I shall therefore be content to make a few remarks on the issues of dissection, organ transplants, genetic engineering, and prolongation of life in the light of Islamic teaching.

Anatomical research in Islam was hampered because human bodies were only occasionally available for dissection. Bodies were sometimes dug up from ancient graveyards and examined, but anatomical research was normally conducted on animals, particularly monkeys and sheep. General religious opinion weighed against permitting the dissection of human bodies on the basis of the dignity of the human body. In pre-Islamic Arab wars, victors in the battlefield sometimes mutilated the bodies of their fallen arch-enemies in order to make an example (*mithāl*) out of them; this vicious practice was called *muthla*. In 625, the battle of Uḥud between Muslims and their Meccan enemies, the wife of the Meccan leader Abū Sufyān, Hind, chewed the heart of Ḥamza, the Prophet's uncle, after an Ethiopian soldier had performed *muthla* on him in the battle field. This practice was proscribed by Islam. Many Muslim jurists considered dissection of a human body to be a kind of *muthla* and advocated its prohibition.

Connected with this is the question of transplanting the organs of a dead person (eyes, heart, and so on) into a living human. Religious opinion was until recently strongly resistant to it and is still largely so. In 1967, when I was director of the Islamic Research Institute of Pakistan, I gave an affirmative answer to a query concerning the transplant of eyes, based upon a classical juristic principle which states "The needs of a living human have priority over those of a dead one."[31] Although an influential daily, *The Dawn* of Karachi, supported the institute's opinion editorially, leading 'Ulama, when questioned on the issue, gave a negative reply. The general community's attitude, however, has been positive on the issue of organ transplants, despite the 'Ulama's disapproval.

The fundamental objection to the manipulation of genes would appear to be that it is "interference with the will of God." Now, the "will of God" often means the "processes of nature uninterfered with by human action." It is, however, commonly accepted that a pregnant woman can improve the health of the fetus by taking certain foods and avoiding others, doing certain exercises, and so on; indeed, certain postures of sexual intercourse have been disapproved by some communities because of fear that the baby would be of unsound health—squint-eyed, for example.[32] If this line of argument is correct, then genetic improvement is highly desirable. Genetic improvement of plant seeds and that of animals has been going on since time immemorial: what objection can there be to the improvement of the human seed—provided, of course, that in the process no loss of human life or human dignity is incurred?

The development of test tube babies is also something to which there could be no Islamic objection, provided the union is between the genes of husband and wife. Indeed, this is a welcome development: it fulfills a genuine need for a child on the part of parents where the mother is unable to conceive the child. The worry that this process is "interference in God's work" is totally unfounded; it is just like the process by which a sapling is cultivated under controlled conditions and transferred to its proper place when it is strong enough to grow there. The worry is not that one is trying to "vie with God" in doing so but rather that one might try to vie with the devil and distort human nature. Islam would not permit the union of genes of a male and a female who are not husband and wife, because this would, it appears, constitute adultery under Islamic law. For under Islamic law, adultery does not mean merely the physical sexual intercourse between an unmarried couple but also refers to a situation where the descent of a child is mixed up—it is partly for this reason that a waiting period (*'idda*) is prescribed by the Qur'an (8, 228; 2, 234) for a divorcee or a widow, in order as far as possible to establish clearly the correct parentage of the child.

Besides, Islamic law, following the Qur'an, had prohibited adoption, along with the pre-Islamic custom of *ẓihār*, as creating false and unnatural relationships. *Ẓihār* was a formula whereby a husband would declare his wife "as inviolate to me as the back [*ẓahr*, meaning "back," but as commentators tell us, actually meaning "front"] of my mother." The Qur'an prohibits both together in 33, 4: "God has not set two hearts in any man's breast. He has not made your wives with whom you do *ẓihār* your mothers, nor has he made your so-called [adopted] sons your real sons. These are [only] words that you utter through your mouths, but God speaks the truth and he guides the right way."

A provision peculiar to Islamic law, "acknowledgment of parenthood" (*al-irrār bi'l-nasab*), may provide the solution to this problem, however. If a boy or girl has no known parentage and is claimed by a man or woman as his or her child, the child shall be assigned to such a claimant. Muhammad al-Shaibānī (d. 804) goes so far as to state that if an unmarried woman goes to the court with a child claiming it to be hers and the child has no other parentage, the court must recognize the woman as the child's mother. The jurists' argument is that in such cases the interest of the child is paramount, and the question of how the child came into being will not be asked. Here principles of equity (*istiḥsān*) and public interest (*maṣlaḥa*) override the strict letter of the law. Al-Shaibānī also states that if a Muslim and a Christian dispute with regard to a boy, the former claiming that the boy belongs to him and is his slave, while the latter claims that the boy is his son and belongs to him, the court must decide in favor of the Christian "because a person's status as a free human has priority over his or her status as a Muslim."[33]

It is obvious, however, that genetic manipulation lays extraordinarily grave responsibility on humans. The most fundamental questions to be asked in this connection are these: What does genetic improvement of the quality of human life mean? Who is authorized to decide? What are the criteria of judgment? The Qur'an says about Saul, "We granted him amplitude of knowledge and physique" (2, 247). This shows that a combination of mental (where mental obviously includes both intellectual and moral qualities) and physical qualities is to be aimed at. But who is to decide upon the nature of these qualities, particularly the moral ones? While there could be in principle no objection to genetic engineering—indeed, it is a welcome opportunity—we know that this unique opportunity also carries with it grave and unprecedented risks. Perhaps it is this fact that renders this opportunity pregnant with both tremendous possibilities and an unprecedented opportunity for moral training and maturity for humankind.

Again, the question of Islam's attitude toward the prolongation of life has never been sufficiently discussed although it must be positive, provided life is healthy and worth living, because for the Qur'an life is meant for "the service of God," for good works. The Qur'an states in several places that old age is unworthy life; it is described as "the worst part of life," because the elderly become forgetful and silly (16, 70; 22, 5). Further, "Whomsoever we give long life, we turn back in the process of creation" (36, 68), that is, an old person becomes like a child, both physically dependent and mentally degenerate. For this reason it would seem that quality of life is to be preferred to quantity of life. Therefore, the prolongation of breathing by artificial life-supports would be strongly disapproved of by the Qur'an. But improvement of the quality of life *along with* its prolongation can only earn the approval of Islam. However, prolonging of good-quality life also demands that food resources and environment must be adjusted for the better because prolongation of life by itself would result in a tremendous increase in population which would exhaust food resources and spoil the environment. Today the question is being asked, "Is death inevitable?" A prior question must be asked, "Is deathless life, as we know it, desirable?"

·6·

Passages

BIRTH

The process of pregnancy and birth is stated in the Qur'an: "We have created man out of an extraction of clay [the origin of semen]; then we turn it into semen and settle it in a firm receptacle. We then turn semen into a clot [literally, something hanging, that is, from the womb] which we then transmute into a lump. We then create bones which we clothe with flesh. Then we transmute it into a new mode [of ensoulment]—blessed be then Allah the best of creators" (23, 12–14; see also 22, 5). The Qur'an thus looks upon the process of the creation of a fetus as a series of genuine transformations or "creations," the last being the "ensoulment." In both passages referred to here, the Qur'an also reminds one of resurrection, which will be another fundamental transformation (re-creation) *on the basis of one's conduct in this world* which is, therefore, organically related to the coming form or level of transformation in the eyes of the Qur'an.

To the formation of the child, both spouses contribute. Although the Qur'an does not say anything on this issue, the Ḥadīth explicitly states that the child is formed from the semen of both the male and female: "The semen of the male being white and that of the female being yellowish."[1] The Ḥadīth is therefore more in line with the Galenic view on the contribution of both the male and the female, although the Ḥadīth does not speak of the female ovaries as Galen does. This is radically different from the Aristotelian doctrine that the male gives the active principle while the female is passive and only provides the place for the activity of the male semen. This doctrine, of course, flows directly from the Aristotelian doctrine (which he applies universally to explain all phenomena) of form and matter, the active and the passive principle, where the passive factor, "the matter," is not something negative, however, but has a positive "tendency" to "become" something, while the active factor, "the form," fashions matter into that something. Although Aristotle believed that the woman contributed only the menstrual blood that fashioned the body of the child and that its soul came from the male, according to the Islamic doctrine the contributions of both spouses produce the entire organism of the child; in a deeper sense, of course, the entire process is the *creation* of God.

In Islamic medical history, Ibn Sīnā, who was basically Aristotelian but had to account for the discovery of the female ovaries, transformed the Galenic theory to fit it into an Aristotelian framework. He believed that it was not just the female menses, but primarily the female semen (which was much more "concocted" that the rest of the menstrual blood) that constituted the effective female contribution to the formation of the fetus. Yet Ibn Sīnā regarded the male semen alone as formative while the female's semen was passive. Ibn Sīnā had to do this, for otherwise the fundamental Aristotelian doctrine of form and matter, as a universal explanatory principle, would be violated. On this issue, however, the Ḥadīth followed its own course based on the principle of the contributions of both male and female. The Prophetic Medicine works, based as they were primarily on Ḥadīth, also followed the same direction. To the question "From what is the child created?" the Prophet is said to have replied, "It is created from both the semen of the man and the semen of the woman. The man's semen is thick and forms the bones and tendons, while the woman's is fine and forms the flesh and blood."[2] The Qur'an, as shown above, states that the body is formed of the male semen. Again, "Let a human see from what he or she has been created. He or she has been created from water that gushes out from between the back and the chest bones" (86, 5–7). The Qur'an, therefore, prima facie would agree more with Aristotle than with Galen, except that it also states, without elaboration, that humankind is created from both male and female (49, 13; cf. 3, 1). Nevertheless, for subsequent theological doctrine, the Ḥadīth was decisive because the Qur'an was held to be less explicit on the matter. Mixed with the Ḥadīth is, of course, the Greek medical tradition, as has been shown by Bāsim Musallam in his *Sex and Society in Islam.*

Before presenting and discussing in some detail the Galen-Aristotle debate on the issue, Ibn Qayyim al Jauzīya, in his *Kitāb al-Tibyān* narrates this Ḥadīth: 'Āyisha and Umm Salmā, two wives of the Prophet, asked him the same question, and in his answer, the Prophet "established the female semen": "Should a woman wash [her clothes] after nocturnal emission [*idhā īḥtalamat*]?" The Prophet said that she should if there is a trace of the fluid. They asked again: "Do women have nocturnal emissions?" The

Prophet retorted, "How else do their children resemble them?" Ibn Qayyim also quotes another version of the Ḥadīth with the following addition: "Do you think that there is any other reason for the resemblance?" Said the Prophet: "When her semen dominates the man's semen the child [boy] will look like her brothers and when the man's semen dominates her semen the child [boy] will look like his brothers."[3]

The principle that the fetus owes itself to both parents' contribution has not had much effect on doctrines of conception control, as we shall see below. But here some important laws may be noted on the status of the fetus and the baby. After the fetus becomes "ensouled," which happens after 120 days of pregnancy, it becomes a "person" in a legal sense, and it has "rights." It may not be aborted, and its abortion counts as homicide. Also, it inherits just as any other living human does, except that until its sex is known, its precise share of inheritance cannot be determined. The actual determination and disposal of inheritance must await birth, in fact, because a pregnancy may result in twins or triplets. Although the Qur'an stresses filial piety for both parents, it is especially tender toward the mother, for "in affliction did she carry him and in affliction did she deliver him" (46, 15). A Ḥadīth from the Prophet says, "The Paradise is under the feet of your mother." For this reason, the Prophet assigned the baby to its mother: "A woman said to the Prophet, 'this son of mine I carried in my womb, I suckled him with my breast and my lap has been his playground, but his father has divorced me and wants to take him away from me!' The Prophet said, 'You have a greater right over him so long as you do not marry.'"[4]

CONTRACEPTION AND ABORTION

Conception control was practiced in pre-Islamic Arabia mostly by *coitus interruptus* (*'azl*). But Ḥadīth is contradictory about whether Islam allows it.[5] There is a Ḥadīth according to which the Prophet said that contraception (*coitus interruptus*) is a "lesser infanticide." But according to another Ḥadīth, a man came to the Prophet and said, "We practice *coitus interruptus*, but we have some Jewish neighbors who say that this is a lesser infanticide." "They are lying," retorted the Prophet. "It is not lesser infanticide; you may practice it, but if God has predetermined for a child to be born, it will be born." After some time, the man reported that his wife had become pregnant, upon which the Prophet said, "Did I not tell you that if a child is predetermined by God to be born it will be born?" It is most probable that neither of these contradictory Ḥadīths emanates from the Prophet but that both arise from a controversy ensuing in Islam after his death, when Arabs conquered neighboring lands and settled in garrison towns. For example, we have the report of a Friday sermon (*khuṭba*), given in Fustāt, the capital and garrison town of Egypt; in his sermon ʻAmr ibn al-ʻĀṣ (d. 663), the governor of Egypt after its conquest, stressed that the Arabs exercise restraint in reproduction.[6] The words of the Qur'an in 4, 3, commonly understood by Muslims to mean "[Marry only one wife], *so that you will likely not go wrong*," have been interpreted by al-Shāfiʻī to mean "so that you will likely not have many children." The words in Arabic (*dhālik adnā an-lā-taʻūlū*) are capable of both interpretations.

There is, however, a third Ḥadīth which seems to have a ring of historical authenticity about it and according to which a companion of the Prophet reported, "We used to practice *coitus interruptus* [during the Prophet's lifetime] and he knew about it while the Qur'an was also being revealed, but the Qur'an did not prohibit it." It therefore seems plausible to hold that the common pre-Islamic practice of contraception was allowed to stand by the Prophet as it was, without his saying anything about it, although it would have been possible for him to ban it, if he had thought fit. The question was, however, consciously raised after him, when some people objected to it on certain grounds. It must be noted first of all that the Qur'an, if it does not command reproduction, nevertheless was understood as encouraging it: "Your women are your tilth," it declares (2, 223). Although it denounces excessive attachment to property and sons as "mere tinsel of this worldly life" (18, 46)—particularly because pagan Arabs set such high priority on them—it nevertheless regards them as blessings of God. But an additional argument was brought by religious leaders to support large-scale reproduction: A Ḥadīth reports the Prophet as saying that, on the Day of Resurrection, he would be proud of the numbers of his community compared with other communities and portrays him as admonishing his followers, "So reproduce and increase in number."[7]

Notwithstanding this general policy statement, many prominent theologians and lawyers permitted contraception and some even abortion within the first four months of pregnancy before the fetus is "infused with life." Such "family planning" was, however, left to individuals and was never adopted as a general social policy.[8] Among the schools of law, the *Ẓāhirī* or the "literalist" school—which had few followers although it had some very prominent jurists, and which is currently rising to prominence in the Arab Middle East—absolutely forbids contraception and abortion. The Shāfiʻī school allows contraception unconditionally *to the husband*, who need not do it with the consent of the wife, for they contend that a wife even if she be free and not a slave has no automatic right to children but only to orgasm. This shows that the biological theory outlined above, according to which both spouses contribute to the generation of the fetus, had little effect on doctrines and laws about contraception, which were essentially based on considerations of social issues. Many lawyers of the other legal schools of Islam allow contraception only with the consent of both spouses, except in the case of a slave-wife. Most considered a slave-wife to be entitled to orgasm but not to ejaculation. According to some, however, the consent of a slave-wife is also necessary, while still others think that the consent of the owner of the slave-wife is necessary and not of the slave-wife because the child would belong to her owner (where the owner is not also the husband): the main reason behind reluctance to reproduce from slave women—and even to marry them—was that their children would also be slaves, which was not desirable.[9]

Among the authorities who allow contraception the most eminent is the Shāfi'ī jurist, theologian, and Sufi al-Ghazālī. Al-Ghazālī held that a truly pious person who has attained to "trust in God" (among the highest spiritual "stations" of Sufism) cannot resort to contraception because he or she *knows* that God, who has created a soul, will not leave it without sustenance. Therefore, for such a person to exercise conception control is *unlawful*. But people who have this kind of trust in God are very rare, while the average person is always haunted by worldly considerations. For such people, it is permitted to exercise conception control to free them of economic worries. Further, if a person fears that having children might force him or her to obtain livelihood by foul means like stealing or robbery, it is *mandatory* that he or she avoid having children in order to avoid the distinct possibility of committing sins. Al-Ghazālī goes so far as to hold that a man who fears that if his wife has children, her health or good looks might be affected *and he might come to dislike her* should refrain from having children.[10]

The impulse to procreate, a pervasive biological need, seems to be especially strong in the East. Particularly sons were considered to be a socioeconomic and moral, if not a biological, necessity. Although it is not so strong in Islam as, for example, in Hinduism, nevertheless, judging from the Qur'an, the Arabs' desire for sons was exceptionally great. This and other social factors coupled with the Prophet's Ḥadīth that Muslims must have large families and that he would be proud of their numbers on the Day of Resurrection, made for a high rate of fertility. Among the important social factors was the fact that generally neither the husband nor the wife had much amusement except each other as well as the fact that sons are regarded as old-age insurance. The number of Muslims in the world is estimated to be around nine hundred million and according to some claims exceeds one billion. The first responsibility of Muslim nations, given these numbers, is to control the flood of population growth, to improve the quality of life, and to distribute the resources of nature more equitably and conscientiously.

Since the 1960s, most Muslim governments have instituted family planning educational programs and have provided facilities to make the programs a success. However, these programs have not been successful. In fact, since March 1984, the government of Pakistan has put a virtual ban on family planning on "moral grounds." This is part of the sociomoral scene in Pakistan since the seizure of power by General Zia Ul-Haq, whose systematically retrogressive policies have almost annihilated the gains made during earlier, more liberal regimes. Khomeini's Iran is, of course, far worse in this respect than Pakistan. Khomeini has sacrificed (and is determined to continue to do so) such large numbers of young boys in the Iran-Iraq war that he can hardly afford to encourage family planning, even if he were inclined to do so (which, of course, he is not). Indeed, the Shi'a practice of *mut'a*, or temporary marriage (banned by Umar I and made unlawful in Sunni Islam, but continued under the Shi'a law as even meritorious), although ignored by the late Shah's government, is getting high priority treatment from Khomeini's government, which has embarked upon a program of systemic "education of the public" in the doctrine and practice of *mut'a*.

As for the moral argument against the use of contraceptives, it is infructuous: it is not the contraceptives themselves that are immoral but their misuse. Family planning, however, is their correct use just as *coitus interruptus* was a correct method to achieve this very end. But if modern contraceptives can be misused for extramarital intercourse so could the *coitus interruptus*. It is, therefore, sheer confusion to regard the presence of modern contraceptive devices as immoral. It is analogous to the argument given by many Muslims which says that the abolition or restriction of polygamy would lead to sexual permissiveness just as in the West monogamy had led to or contributed to it. It is true that during the recent decades there has been increasing sexual permissiveness in the West, but it is not at all certain that monogamy had led to it or contributed to it materially. Nor is there any factual evidence nor any claim on the part of the Qur'an that polygamy confers any immunity from sexual deviancy. The ban on contraceptives imposed in Pakistan is apparently based on the legal-moral concept of "blocking the way to sin" (*sadd al-dharā'i'*) propounded by classical Muslim lawyers. This doctrine means that not only must sin be prevented but also the path or means to it must be blocked. It is on this basis that many religous leaders in the latter part of the 1900s and early decades of this century sought to prevent the public education of women; once women went beyond the protective four walls of the house, it was believed, their chastity would be threatened. This principle, although it does have a sound point, is obviously often taken to absurd lengths: when pushed far enough, its logic would require that one live on the mountains rather than in the cities where opportunities for sin abound. There are really no legal provisions sufficient to create a bulwark against errancy if the moral fiber is not strong enough, and, given strong moral training, legal defenses do not count for much.

In the Muslim countries, the only program acknowledged to be effective by the United Nations is that of Indonesia, although reports of the United Nations depend on the data supplied by the governments of the countries being studied. When I worked in Pakistan and was connected with the religious aspects of the implementation of the program for family planning (1964–68), my study showed that theological aspects were of limited importance. Of course, officials sought to bolster their policies with the opinions of religious authorities like al-Ghazālī, while the opposition exploited the opposite opinions. But I found those arguments were relevant only to the urban middle class and especially the lower middle classes, whose education was not high but who could read well enough to be largely influenced by the religious opposition to the family planning campaign. The higher middle and upper classes were generally convinced of the utility and even necessity of population control. But the bulk of the population lives in the countryside; there, as a matter of fact, peasants understood the force of the *economic* argument if it was cogently put forward, and the available evidence suggested that the program was fairly effective in places where it had been well communicated.

In the Muslim world as a whole, two types of religious opinions exist and work at two levels. The higher 'Ulama, who have a solid base in religious learning, generally allow family planning as an individual family's decision but strongly oppose it as an official policy. This is connected with a widespread belief, political in nature, that the idea of population control has originated in the West, which is frightened by the rising tide of the Third World population and therefore wants to control its growth. This argument has had powerful appeal on the urban masses in Third World countries and effectively counteracts official policies where they exist. "A child born in the United States," people are told, "consumes twenty times the resources a child in the Third World does." For every American child, then, the Third World can afford twenty. The moral overtones of the argument are obvious.

It has often been held that no policy of population control can be effective unless abortion is legalized, as in Japan. According to the 1969 United Nations estimate, the Japanese population was declining at a rate which if continued, would render the Japanese race extinct in three hundred years. But in the past decade, Japanese population has registered an increase, probably due to the extraordinary pace of industrialization. In Islam, as said above, several medieval jurists had permitted abortion within four months of pregnancy before the fetus was "ensouled," although the majority opposed it because the fetus was "going to be ensouled" and the coming into being of new life was not, therefore, a remote possibility but a ripe potentiality which could not be destroyed. A policy like the one adopted by the current Chinese Communists, under which mature fetuses are aborted under official aegis, will never succeed in Islam. But all this means that *individuals* have to be made conscious of what is at stake *for them* primarily, and only secondarily for the collective existence of Muslims, and that there is no conflict between the two but, rather, a coalescing of both interests. There does exist, it seems, the possibility of general acceptance of abortion within four months of pregnancy, which will go a long way in making population control effective.[11]

SEXUALITY

"We have created everything in pairs" (51, 49), says the Qur'an, which here and elsewhere leaves the strong impression that sex represents a universal law. Sex in humans, therefore, is only a special case of this universal phenomenon. Nevertheless, human sex life exhibits characteristics that are unique in the animal kingdom: the institution of marriage and the family. Pre-Islamic Arabia had an institution of "free love" (*khidn*, plural *akhdān*, "partners in free love") which the Qur'an terminated (4, 25; 5, 5) in favor of the marital arrangement. The Qur'anic legislation introduced and insisted upon the concept of chastity (*iḥṣān*), a state of sexual "immunity" supposed to be induced into spouses by marriage to a single partner. For this state of sexual immunity, therefore, males do not need more than one wife. The opposite state of "living in sin" was characterized as "lewdness" (*sifāḥ*) and was forbidden.

There is a vast ocean of literature in Islam on the theme of sexuality ranging from crass physicalism to the expression of the most refined and sublime sentiments and thoughts. Pre-Islamic Arabic poetry (the teaching of which was assiduously cultivated in the Islamic educational system because of its affinity to the Qur'anic idiom and style) already contained both strands, the crass and the refined—but without the spiritual element which was contributed later by Sufism.[12] In the popular medical literature of Islam, sexual aphrodisiac prescriptions invariably form a prominent part; such literature, particularly in the Subcontinent, was influenced by the Hindu *Kāma Sūtra*, or *The Science of Sex.*[13]

I have already hinted that while some Sufis like al-Hujwīrī were misogynists, the average Sufi married and had a family life. In Sufi thought and emotion, woman played a very important role, sometimes highly flattering and sometimes not at all flattering. The latter is projected most tellingly in the oft-expressed Sufi doctrine that a person who goes through the path of Sufi spiritual itinerary is a *fatā*, a *chevalier*, which is pre-eminently a male role. The Sufi 'Aṭṭār (d. 1190) states that when a woman becomes a Sufi, she becomes a *fatā* and ceases to be a woman! Annemarie Schimmel has quoted the Indian Sufi Jamāl Hānswī as saying, "The seeker of this world is a female, the seeker of the other world is an hermaphrodite, while the seeker of the Lord is masculine."[14] However, the basic Islamic equality of the two sexes leads most Sufis to make no sex distinction at the spiritual level. Ibn 'Arabī (d. 1240), for example—and in this Ibn 'Arabī is no different from an average Sufi—regards it as quite normal that a woman should attain to the highest spiritual goals as a man does. In fact, in the later phase of Sufism, roughly from the twelfth century on, sex-symbolism played an extremely important role, following the alleged Ḥadīth of the Prophet "From this world of yours God has made two things dear to me, women and scent, while my spiritual elevation is in prayers."

Ibn 'Arabī, who believed that God is both masculine and feminine, also believed that Adam and Eve both partook of both sexes. A very curious passage from this highly enigmatic and extraordinarily influential Sufi's magnum opus, *al-Futūḥāt al-Makkīya* (Meccan Disclosures) reads:

> From this knowledge [that is, intuitive knowledge which comes from God's light rather than discursive reason] we know that women are exact moieties of men. Do you not see that Eve was created from Adam? Thus she possesses [like Adam] two characteristics, being masculine in her origin and principle and feminine derivatively. Thus, her nature [like that of Adam] is ambiguous. All humanity is thus a mélange of masculinity and femininity. Otherwise we cannot conceive the nature of the agent in relation to that of the patient which is the recipient from the agent, since such agent cannot act except upon something that is [basically] similar to it. This is so because the agent first produces in itself the passiv-

ity whereby the form of that to which it develops passivity appears in it [that is, the form of that upon which it subsequently acts first appears in its mind and acts upon it]. Through that power [of conception] that which is passive becomes passive to it. It is thus that he [God] becomes the Creator, the Producer, and the Truly Real [that is, by conceiving creatures in his mind].

We have already explained while investigating knowledge vis à vis the knower that knowledge follows upon the object of knowledge while it itself is an attribute of the knower and that it gives [to the knower] the knowledge of the object as it is. Then the knower gives external existence to the object of knowledge, just as the Creator gives external existence to the object of creation and brings it into being.

From this can be known the reason why God made women dear to [the Prophet] Muhammad (God's peace and blessings be upon him). So whosoever loves women with the kind of love that the Prophet had for them, indeed, loves God. The essence of the matter is the passivity whereby the object of knowledge [acting upon the mind of the knower] gives him knowledge whereby he is said to be the knower. Thus the knower is in the first place passive to the object of knowledge. This kind of passivity relates Jesus to Mary, a case parallel to that of Eve vis à vis Adam—*therein lies the admonition for one who possesses a mind* [Qur'an 50, 37], so that he may understand the words of God the Almighty [Qur'an 49, 13], "O Mankind! We have created you from a male and a female"—that is, like Eve and Jesus respectively, and, through the combination of Adam's children, all the rest of mankind. The feminine [principle] thus comprehends the creation of all mankind.

When I first joined the Path [of Sufism] I had the utmost hate for women and I refrained from sex relations for about eighteen years, until I discovered this spiritual station. I became frightened over my misogyny, when I understood [the meaning of] the Ḥadīth according to which the Prophet (God's peace be upon him) had been *made by* God to love women, so that he did not love them by [physical] nature but rather by God's *causing* him to love them. When I truly and sincerely concentrated upon God [seeking light] on this matter, since I was frightened of God's possible anger because I hated what God had made dear to his Prophet, God delivered me for which he be praised—and made me love women. Now, I have the utmost kindness among all creation for them and I am most regardful of them—since I have now truly understood the matter. This love of mine is not through any physical passion but because God has caused me to do so.[15]

Circumcision is universally practiced among Muslims in the case of male children and is described in the Ḥadīth as being "according to nature." Some Ḥadīth asserts that the prophet Abraham was the first of men to be circumcised. It is thus regarded as a sunna of the Prophet Muhammad but is in practice like an obligatory duty. The Ḥanafī school of law does not accept the circumcision of girls (clitoridectomy), but other schools of Sunni law accept it just as they accept boys' circumcision. Practically all major works of Sunni Ḥadīth accept the report according to which the Prophet said, "When the circumcised organ [of the male] touches the circumcised organ [of the female], taking bath becomes mandatory," which shows that circumcision of girls must have been an old practice. Today, clitoridectomy is common in Sudan and Egypt.

In Islam the wife has the inalienable right to sexual satisfaction, and the Prophet is reported to have granted divorce to a woman on grounds of her husband's impotency *when she complained.*[16] According to some Ḥadīth reports, making love to one's wife is even counted as a meritorious act, for if, instead of committing the sexual act in the right place, one had done it in the wrong place, one would have earned God's wrath and punishment.[17] I have already referred to the verse of the Qur'an which says, "Women are tilth for you, so approach your tilth in whatever way you like" (2, 223). This is interpreted to mean prohibition of approaching women in the hind because that stultifies her function of reproduction. Although all other methods of coitus are thus allowed in this verse, lawyers encourage only such postures as are conducive to full and satisfactory ejaculation and to the conception of the baby. This would tend to discourage the practice of *coitus interruptus* which, however, is allowed, as we have seen, for the purpose of contraception *if it is called for.*

The Qur'an has fixed the maximum suckling period at two years, although it can be cut off earlier by the mutual consent of the parents. The Prophet is reported to have said, "I was thinking of prohibiting suckling a baby while the woman is pregnant, but I have seen the Persians and Byzantines do this and it does not harm their children"—that is, it does not harm the fetus. This has been interpreted to mean that the practice should be discouraged, which in turn has been taken to mean that, as far as possible, contraception should be resorted to while a baby is being suckled. Suckling also affects relations from the point of view of marriage. A woman who has suckled a child becomes its foster-mother, although no inheritance rights are created. A boy and a girl who have suckled the milk of the same woman are prohibited from marrying each other, but their brothers and sisters who have not suckled the woman's milk incur no such disability. The amount of milk suckled that creates such prohibition is a subject on which views differ, but "three sucklings" is regarded by most as the minimum for creating prohibition. The rationale is that since milk is produced by blood, suckling creates consanguinity.

"They ask you concerning menstruation," says the Qur'an (2, 222), "Say

(O Muhammad!), menstruation is a disability, so keep away [from sexual intercourse with] women during menstruation until they are cleansed and when they are cleansed, go unto them as God as bidden you to do—indeed, God loves those who turn to him in repentance and he loves the pure." Menstruation thus requires abstention from sexual intercourse, but the woman is not otherwise "boycotted" during menstruation. The Ḥadīth warns against sexual intercourse during menstruation, but the law prescribes no penalties for offense except repentance as the Qur'an has asked for. Women are asked not to pray or fast during menstruation, and this absolution was tendentiously used in Ḥadīth to prove women's "inferiority in religion," as discussed above.

Masturbation is disapproved of, but no legal penalties exist. Medical literature in Islam disapproves of it on physical grounds, namely, that it leads to impotency in males. There is hardly any discussion of it in religious literature.

Homosexuality is forbidden in law. In the Qur'an the practice is condemned as indulged in by the people of Lot, a crime for which they were destroyed. The story recurs in the Qur'an but is discussed specially in 11, 76. In 7, 80, the Qur'an asserts that the people of Lot committed homosexuality in an unprecedented manner or on an unprecedented scale. The heinousness of the crime is said to consist in the fact that it "obstructs the path" (29, 29) of procreation. On the penalty, there are differences of opinion. Some hold that it equals that of illicit heterosexual intercourse, while others regard it as a lesser crime. The Qur'an's dictum concerning a penalty is uncertain. In 4, 15–16 we read, "Those of your women who commit obscenity, bring as witnesses thereupon four of you; should they give evidence against them, keep them in their homes until death comes to them or God provides for them some [other] way out. And those two of you who commit obscenity, punish them moderately . . . but if they repent and reform themselves, leave them alone, for God indeed returns [to the penitent] and is merciful." Some commentators see those two verses as referring to homosexuality among females and males respectively, for in the first verse, only women are referred to while in the second the relative dual pronoun used, "those two," is in the masculine gender. Most hold, however, that both verses are talking about illicit heterosexual intercourse and that the masculine dual pronoun can, in common Arabic usage, refer to a pair, that is, a male and a female. Many of these latter believe, however, that the verses do cover both heterosexual and homosexual intercourse. It is commonly held that this was an interim solution for both crimes, a solution later replaced by one hundred lashes in 24, 2: "As for the adulteress and the adulterer, flog each of them with one hundred lashes and let not soft-heartedness take hold of you in implementing the religion of God, and let a group of the faithful witness their punishment." The view has also been held that the words *adulteress* and *adulterer* in this verse do not refer to persons who may have slipped but to those who indulge habitually in whoredom. This seems to be corroborated by the following verse (24, 3) which says, "A whore-monger shall not marry except a whore or an idolatress, and none shall marry a whore except a whore-monger or an idolator—it is forbidden to the faithful [to do so]."

In order to prove adultery, fornication, or homosexual intercourse, four witnesses are demanded by the Qur'an. If a person alleges such intercourse against someone, particularly a woman (24, 4), and does not come forth with four witnesses, he or she is to be given eighty lashes. That person's evidence will be unacceptable in a court henceforth—unless he or she repents. This demand proved a great deterrent against reports or allegations of illicit sexual intercourse. If a husband alleges adultery by his wife but has not witnesses, then he must take a solemn oath four times and the fifth time he must say, "God's curse be upon me if I am lying." If the wife does the same, swears to her chastity four times and says the fifth time, "God's curse be upon me if he [my husband] is right," she will not be punished, but the bond of marriage shall stand legally severed.

Notwithstanding the Qur'anic penalty of one hundred lashes, apparently for both adultery and fornication—the Qur'an does not make any distinction between the two—a radical change occurred in law on the basis of Ḥadīth, which, on the alleged authority of the Prophet, restricted the Qur'anic punishment to fornication and prescribed death by stoning for an adulterer.[18] Since it is inconceivable that the Prophet himself would have introduced such a radical change in a Qur'anic measure, it is highly likely that this was done later by the caliph 'Umar I, for it was in his time that, after rapid conquests and a massive increase in the number of the prisoners of war, including slave women, Mecca and Medina experienced tremendous sexual chaos, as is also witnessed by 'Umar's legislation on the subject of women slaves.[19] It was also 'Umar, who, as we have seen in the preceding chapter, introduced the law that if a man divorces his wife by a "triple repudiation" formula, she would be irrevocably divorced without any opportunity for reconciliation or remarriage unless the wife first marries someone else and he either divorces her or dies. These are all indications of the extent to which 'Umar I exerted himself to control the sexual chaos that resulted from the superabundance of foreign women.

But because the penalty for adultery was so severe, like certain other

Qur'anic penalties called *ḥudūd* (singular *ḥadd*, which, in law, means a punishment that cannot be increased or decreased from the quantity prescribed by the Qur'an, for example, cutting off of a hand for theft), the jurists defined the crime so narrowly and fixed the evidence requirements so stringently that it became practically inoperative. Adultery/fornication/homosexual intercourse was defined as the actual physical penetration, and to prove it four *eye-witnesses* were required by law (the Qur'an had required four witnesses, not eye-witnesses). Short of self-confession, therefore, there was no way to prove illicit sexual intercourse, and confession was required to be repeated three times with considerable time-intervals. As a result, even if the accused confessed twice, he or she could retract the confession on the third occasion. The Shi'a do not accept the validity of the *ḥadd*-punishments unless the iman's rule is there; under Khomeini's rule, these penalties are now being given generously.

Besides, Islamic law makes certain provisions for the legitimization of children, even though the fundamental law on the issue remains that a child is legitmate only if it is born at least six months after wedlock. I mentioned one provision in Chapter 5: the law of acknowledgment of parenthood. Another provision is expressed in the legal maxim "The child belongs to the matrimonial bed," which is based on alleged Ḥadīths from the Prophet. According to one Ḥadīth, a Bedouin came to the Prophet and said, "My wife has given birth to a black boy, and I cannot recognize him as my son." The Prophet asked him the color of his camels and he replied that they were red. The Prophet then asked him whether he had any with brown color, to which he replied in the affirmative. When the Prophet asked from where he thought some got brown color, the Bedouin said they must have taken after some distant male ancestor. The Prophet then said that perhaps the child too had taken after some distant ancestor of his, and he did not permit the Bedouin to disavow the child.[20]

Another example is even more radical. The wife of the Prophet 'Āyisha relates that 'Utba ibn Abī Waqqāṣ once said to his more illustrious brother Sa'd ibn Abī Waqqāṣ (a companion of the Prophet who conquered Iran under 'Umar I) that he had once cohabited with a slave-girl of Zam'a and had a son from that slave-girl, adding that he was authorizing his brother Sa'd to take the boy. When Mecca fell to Islam, Sa'd got hold of the boy, saying that he was taking back his brother's son. But the older son of Zam'a, 'Abd, claimed that the slave-girl's son was his true stepbrother. Both claimants went before the Prophet, Sa'd claiming that the boy was his brother's son who had been given to him, while 'Abd said, "He is my brother, he is son of my father's slave-girl and *was born on his bed.*" The Prophet gave the boy to 'Abd saying, "He [is your brother and] belongs to you because the *child belongs to the* [*matrimonial*] *bed* and the adulterer must get death by lapidation." The crucially important point in this Ḥadīth comes when the Prophet says to Sauda, 'Abd's real sister, "You must not see any more of the boy," when he noticed the remarkable similarity of the boy under dispute with 'Utba, his real father. The Prophet, however, still went on to say to 'Abd, "The boy *is* your brother and belongs to you for he was born on your father's [cohabitational] bed."[21] Thus although on the basis of "scientific" evidence, that is, clear physical appearance, the boy should have been given to Sa'd as his brother's son, the Prophet still gave it to his putative father's son while asking the latter's sister to segregate herself from him, with which they both complied.

The harsh penalties of crimes like adultery and theft were then largely mitigated through juristic manipulation of their definitions and the laws of evidence. However, it is possible to take a sociological approach to the interpretation of these punishments that would be more direct and honest than the classical jurists' manipulation. The Arab tribal society, which forms the background of these punishments, had an extraordinarily heightened sense of personal honor (*'irḍ*), as noted above. Adultery gravely violated the honor of the woman, her family, and especially her husband. But theft was also regarded as a serious violation of personal honor.[22] Thus, a person whose valuable property was stolen claimed not only that he was deprived of an economic asset but that he had been dishonored. And the punishment for the invasion of personal honor was quite harsh. With the change of society from a tribal to an urban one, however, the concept of honor necessarily changes its dimension and the punishments must be adjusted accordingly.

DEATH

Suicide is forbidden in Islamic law. There is no direct and explicit text in the Qur'an or Ḥadīth on the issue, but there are texts which assume the prohibition of taking one's own life: "And spend in the cause of God [spend on the poor segments of society] *and do not cast yourselves into destruction*" (Qur'an 2, 195). The direct meaning of the verse is that withholding expenditure on the poor ones of the community will eventually mean self-destruction of the community. The idea assumes, however, that putting oneself into perdition is evil.

Similarly, the Qur'an (4, 29) says, "Do not kill yourselves," whose direct meaning has been taken to be "do not kill each other." This in turn is taken to assume that a Muslim's killing another Muslim is tantamount to killing himself or herself. According to Islamic law, God is the creator of life; therefore, a person does not "own" his or her life and hence cannot terminate it. The only way a Muslim can and is expected to freely give and take life is "in the path of Allah," as a martyr in *jihād*. According to a Ḥadīth a person who dies defending self, family, and property (by extension also the country) against aggression is also a martyr. The incidence of suicide in the Muslim community is so rare as to be negligible.

I have emphasized the Qur'anic view that resurrection and judgment are central in the divine scheme for humans and that the nature of the future life of a person depends on his or her performance *in this life*, in the span between birth and death or, more accurately, between adulthood and death. For the Qur'an, the after-death life is as concrete and palpable as the "life in this world": there is a natural continuity between the two, and death is the passage between them. The Qur'an recurrently and untiringly emphasizes the unlimited mercy and forgiveness of God, but it links a person's future with his or her performance here. Consistently with this, it categorically disallows intercession as well as repentance on deathbed when there is no more opportunity for a person to work and earn. Pharaoh, when he saw he was drowning in the Red Sea, repented of his sins, but God said to him, "Now [you repent]! while you have been disobedient [to God] all along and were among the corrupters [of the earth]?" (10, 91). Even more categorically, "Acceptance of repentance by God is only for those who commit evil out of inadvertence and then soon repent—these are the ones to whom God returns and God is knowing and wise. Repentance is not for those who continuously commit evil until when death comes to one of them he says, "Now I repent . . ." (4, 17–18).

As for intercession, the Qur'an raises the issue several times but seems to deny it. Among the most categorical verses is 2, 254: "O you who believe! Spend [on the poor] of what we have given you by way of wealth before the day comes when there shall be no trade-offs, nor any friendships, nor any intercession." In view of God's infinite mercy, this appears to be a consistent stand. Yet Ḥadīth is full of intercession of all prophets on behalf of the sinners of their communities and particularly of Muhammad's sweepingly successful intercession on behalf of his community. In popular belief, saints, especially the putative head of the ubiquitous Qādirī order of Sufis, 'Abd al-Qādir al-Jīlānī (d. 1166), outstrip all prophets. The orthodoxy, once it decided to adopt intercession, imported it also into the Qur'an by suitably interpreting several verses of the Qur'an which say that none will be able to intercede with God "except by his permission" (2, 255; 21, 28; 10, 3) and ignoring other verses where the Qur'an insists that God alone is the intercessor (6, 51, 70; 32, 4). Belief in intercession, coupled with the important Ḥadīth (discussed above) that a person who professes there is no God but Allah will go to paradise even if he or she committed adultery and theft, was bound to lower moral tension.

On the other hand, other developments counter-balanced such a sense of complacency, mainly the introduction of the doctrine of the "chastisement in the grave" imported from Zoroastrianism in Iran. The idea that a dead person does not have to await the Day of Judgment to receive rewards and punishment but begins his reckoning in the grave does not exist in the Qur'an but abounds in the Ḥadīth. Doors of hell or heaven are opened to the deceased, in accordance with their deserts, while they are yet in the grave. According to a well-known Ḥadīth, "Judgment begins immediately upon death." This "intermediary stage" (*barzakh*) between this life and the actual resurrection is a foretaste of things to come. This doctrine was apparently accepted by Islam in order to bring judgment immediately after a person's death since the Day of Judgment was in an unknowable future.

The entirety of the Qur'an is directed toward inculcating in human beings a sense of piety or moral responsibility called *taqwā*, which literally means "to protect oneself" (against moral peril). *Taqwā* is an instrument or an inner power which enables one to discriminate between right and wrong *and to judge one's own actions.* Ordinarily, people fail to judge their own actions properly because of deep layers of self-deception and self-righteousness such that even human conscience becomes colored by them. According to the Qur'an, therefore, "the weighing of deeds" that will take place on the Day of Judgment will necessarily entail self-recognition by a person of the "real" worth of his or her deeds as opposed to the worth the person assigned to them during the lifetime. If, therefore, men and women can develop proper *taqwā* in this life and see themselves for what they really are, there *will be no need for the Day of Judgment*, for every moment of life will be the Hour of Judgment.

Death for the Qur'an, then, is a mere link or a passage between two segments of a continuous life: "God receives the souls when they die and those who do not die he receives them in their sleep; he then keeps those for whom he has decreed death while others he releases until the appointed term ..." (39, 42). The analogy of sleep with death here is supposed to refer to two common elements: in both cases consciousness is abrogated, and both intervene between two periods of wakefulness or return of consciousness. In 6, 60 we are told, "it is he who takes you by night and he knows what you do during the day; he raises you up again by day so you may complete your appointed term. You will all return to him and then he will tell you what you had been doing." Sleep, therefore, is a sort of lesser death.

Further, this transition or passage of death is portrayed by the Qur'an as being a difficult experience for the wicked, probably because they did not believe in an afterlife, the only life they knew was coming to an end, and this they had spent in evilmongering. "If you could but see [how it will be] when these evilmongers find themselves in the agonies of death, and the angels stretch forth their hands [and call], 'give up your inner selves. To-day you shall be requited with the suffering of humiliation for having attributed to God something that is not true and for having persistently scorned his messengers in your arrogance'" (6, 93). In fact, those who had rejected the truth would undergo torture even at the time of death: "If you could but see [how it is] when angels take the lives of those who rejected the truth and they strike their faces and back [and say to them], 'Taste the burning torture. This is because of your own life-performance, for God does not tyrannize over his servants'" (8, 50–51).

When a person is dying, relatives and close friends are normally present. Because Islam recognizes no intermediaries between humans and God, it has, strictly speaking, no clergy. Not even the Sufis, who claimed to look after the spiritual life of their followers (as opposed to the purely legal and doctrinal aspects of religious life which were the task of the 'Ulama), could claim to mediate on behalf of the dying by administering sacraments. As said above, repentance on deathbed is unacceptable in Islam. The dying person recites the confession of the faith. "There is no god but God and Muhammad is his messenger." If he or she has done some wrong to anyone, the forgiveness of that person is sought, if possible, for according to Islamic doctrine, "Fulfilling the rights of people has priority over the rights of God, and God will not forgive violation of human rights unless those wronged have forgiven."[23]

Islam encourages attending funeral services as a meritorious act whether those who participate in the service personally knew the deceased or not. Indeed, if a person known for piety or a great leader of Islam dies, funeral services are held in several places even though the body, of course, is present in only one place. This funeral service *in absentia* is regarded as spiritually beneficial both for the dead and for those who participate in the service. The Prophet's traditions enjoin burial of the dead without unnecessary delay, burial rights being simple and austere. Wailing loudly for the dead is forbidden, probably as a reaction to the pre-Islamic Arab custom according to which the death of important people like tribal chiefs and war-heroes was announced far and wide by professional announcers (*nāʿī*) and wailing was an important ritual performed by women. In most Muslim societies, particularly in the countryside, the wailing ritual for big landlords or important men is still performed. Again, although Islamic doctrine strictly forbids wailing for the dead or observance of their death beyond three days,[24] in most Muslim societies pre-Islamic customs still prevail: in fact, for both marriages and deaths, the simple rules of Islam are largely ignored and elaborate ceremonies held. A ceremony is observed universally in Muslim countries on the third and often also on the fortieth day after the death of a dear one; the Qur'an-recitation *in completo* is done, and guests who participate in the recitations are given food. A spectacular illustration of the reverence for the pious dead—despite the Islamic doctrine that the human body "turns to dust and only a person's meritorious deeds remain forever"—is afforded by an incident at the death of the aforementioned theologian-jurist Ibn Taimīya (d. 1328) in a prison at Damascus. All his life, Ibn Taimīya had relentlessly fought against the superstitions of popular Islam, which had been carried on and encouraged by popular forms of Sufism. His final imprisonment, wherein he died, was in fact occasioned by his opinion expressed in a *fatwa* (authoritative verdict) that it was wrong to undertake a journey for the express purpose of visiting a grave, including the grave of the Prophet. (The current Saudi Islam is patterned largely on Ibn Taimīya's teachings.) When, however, his body was being carried through the streets of Damascus from the prison to his grave, women stood on roofs of their homes and threw down their scarves in order to touch his bier and acquire spiritual merit—something he had condemned all his life!

EPILOGUE

The previous pages have revealed to us that health concerns and medicine in Islam were shot through with a religio-ethical motivation and valuation and that healing the sick was generally regarded as the highest form of "service to God" after the religiously prescribed rituals. This religious motivation also set into motion certain processes, theoretical and practical, that were the spiritual and cultural backbone of the entire Islamic medical institution. The theoretical development was the corpus of Ḥadīth attributed to the Prophet on medicine, whereas the practical phenomenon was the *auqāf* or the pious foundations that proliferated throughout the world of Islam, some small and some very large, indeed, to support health institutions. It should be remembered that the *auqāf* for health, although founded by governments, nobles, and other rich persons, were *religious* institutions just like those founded for other religious purposes like mosques, *madrasas*, and Sufi hospices.

But when, in 1838, the Ottoman sultan Maḥmūd II inaugurated the first modern (that is, Western-style) medical school and hospital in Istanbul, staffed by French doctors, claiming that the Islamic medical tradition had become stagnant and sterile, one could clearly see that the wind of secularization had begun to blow hard. The extent of this change can be measured by certain statements contained in the sultan's inaugural address. He said, for instance, that the corpus of Islamic medicine was (primarily) enshrined in the Arabic language, which was difficult for Turks to master; now, of course, it *had to* become easy for the Turks to learn French—and, in any case, why could Arabic medical works (along with French and others) not be translated into Turkish?

Other Muslim countries sooner or later went the same way. Throughout the nineteenth and twentieth centuries modern medical institutions grew and multiplied in the Muslim world, the old tradition having been officially sent to limbo. In the twenties of the present century, Reza Khan, shah of Iran, went so far in his zeal for modernization (often imitating Mustafa Kemal the Ataturk) that he even banned the practice of traditional medicine and actually imprisoned some of its practitioners. It was only in the Subcontinent, which came under direct British rule, that the traditional systems of medicine (Muslim and Hindu) survived. In Pakistan in the mid-sixties, the government of Muhammad Ayub Khan even ordered the official registration and licensing of traditional *ḥakīms* (much to the chagrin of modern physicians) because modern medical services are highly expensive and scarcely available in the countryside. In more recent years, a tremendous brain-drain of the Third World has occurred in the medical field because of the large-scale immigration of doctors there to America and Europe. This exodus was particularly acute from Egypt during Nasser's regime and seems to have climaxed from Iran after Khomeini's takeover.

The basic question, however, is: why can the modern medicine not be acculturated into Islam just as in the earlier centuries? Muslims were able to acculturate Greek, Persian, and Indian medical traditions into Islam and thus provide it with a spiritual home just as they did with the other traditions in the past. For the Prophetic, or at least putatively Prophetic, authority is still there, of which, in fact, a good deal has been added by subsequent authorities. So far, though, the modern medical tradition has remained "in the cold" without enjoying the warmth of the cultural home in spiritual terms; it remains both secular and materialistic in its moral nature and purpose. In its financial backing, it is relentlessly secular. And here lies a great irony, for Muslims claim, and often claim vociferously, that Islam regards all fields of human activity—public as well as private—as Islamic and that it therefore cannot recognize any activity as secular. I think this is correct. Yet the modern medical professions (and others, including almost the entire governmental activity) are secular, despite the Qur'an's provision of the laws of *zakāt* (9, 60), which were intended to render all spheres of the state properly Islamic. This law mentions as categories of *zakāt* expenditure *all* the expenditures of a modern welfare state, including money for (1) the poor, (2) the wages or salaries of those who collect the *zakāt* tax (this was the only civil service in the Prophet's days, but today it must include the entire civil service), (3) diplomatic expenditure for "those whose hearts are to be won for Islam," (4) ransoming of war-captives, (5) relieving the debts of those under chronic debt, (6) "the cause of Allah," which the Qur'an commentators tell us means defense and works of social ministry such as education and health, and (7) "[to provide facilities] for the travelers, that is communications."

By some ironic turn of legal interpretation which perverted the entire teaching of the verse, the *zakāt* was practically restricted to the first category, the poor; *religious* education was also accommodated. If the Muslims can rethink the law of *zakāt* and interpret the above verse in contemporary terms, the whole financial system can and, indeed, *must* become Islamic. But Muslims are unable to do this because of the sheer weight of conservatism, for conservatism pulls the attention of Muslims entirely to *the tradition as it has been built up* and away both from the Qur'an and from contemporary needs and demands. Recently, a few Muslim countries, particularly Iran and Pakistan, have reinstated *zakāt* as an official tax after it had lapsed into a private charity for a long time, particularly under Western colonial rule. But no Muslim nation has been able to reconstruct *zakāt* as a full-blown tax adequate for all state needs, as the Qur'an explicitly requires; it has remained expressly restricted to the needs of the poor or, to an extent, to "religious" education—despite the fact that Muslims continue to deny the dualism between religious and secular education (which they accuse Christianity of having created!).

Since Muslims have neither invested modern medicine with moral-spiritual values and motivation nor yet created proper and adequate financial bases for it, this tradition has remained so far quite infertile and unoriginal. The financial bases were adequate in medieval ages because, first, medieval research was not on such a vast scale as it is in modern times, and second, Muslims had large areas of unified rule—the Baghdad caliphate, which was succeeded by the Ottoman, the Mogul, and the Safavid empires. Today the Muslim world is split up into relatively small countries with insufficient resources, and some "countries" like the Gulf shaikhdoms are artificial and ridiculously small. Unless Muslim countries can pool their resources and cooperate to develop a moral-spiritual élan for promoting medical concerns, they must remain uncreative imitators of the West. For one major difference between the medieval and modern times from our particular perspective is that in the medieval centuries Muslims were ascendant—politically, economically, and as a civilization—relative to the peoples (Greeks and Persians) who had suffered a decline, whereas at the present the West has been ascendant for some two centuries while the Muslim world has been at a low ebb. Only since the forties have Muslims gradually gained independence from Western colonialism at least *politically*. But culturally they are still under the dominance of the West.

In 1969, Muslim countries created an association of Muslim states called the Organization of Islamic Conference (OIC) with its headquarters in Jedda, Saudi Arabia. They have set up committees and commissions for cooperation, but in the medical field nothing has emerged so far. If a breakthrough is to occur in this extremely important area, it is necessary that OIC members devise ways and means for a close cooperation.

Notes

Chapter 1/Wellness and Illness in the Islamic World View

1. The following account of God, nature, humankind, and society is more or less a brief summary of my *Major Themes of the Qur'ān* (Minneapolis: Bibliotheca Islamica, 1980), chaps. 1, 2, and 3.
2. Ernest Renan, "L'Islamisme et la Science," *Oeuvres Completes de Ernest Renan* (Paris, 1947–61), 1:950. Renan intended by this story to show that Islam, as a religion, is an enemy of science, philosophy, and progress. But the Turkish writer Namik Kemal, in his "Reply to Renan" (in *Kullīyāt* [Istanbul, 1908], 1:28–29), points out that this very event proves the liberalism, open-mindedness, and tolerance of Islam.
3. On Ḥadīth (traditions from the Prophet) and Sunna (Prophetic example), see *Encyclopaedia of Islam*, new ed., s.v. "Ḥadīth." Further references are given there.
4. See Fazlur Rahman, *Islamic Methodology in History* (Karachi, 1965), p. 160.
5. See the famous anthology of Sunni Ḥadīth titled *Mishkāt al-Maṣābīḥ* (Delhi, 1955), p. 23. It has been translated into English by James Robson, 4 vols. (Lahore, 1960–65); this quotation appears in 1:26. (Subsequent references to the *Mishkāt* will cite Robson's translation in parentheses.)
6. See the work of Shi'a Ḥadīth, *al-Kāfi* (Tehran, 1961), 1:155ff.
7. For a general history of Sufism, see A. J. Arberry, *Sufism* (London, 1950); also I. Spencer Trimmingham, *The Sufi Orders in Islam* (Oxford: Oxford University Press, 1971), and Fazlur Rahman, *Islam* (Chicago: University of Chicago Press, 1979), chaps. 8, 9.
8. English translation by W. Montgomery Watt, *Faith and Practice of al-Ghazali* (London, 1953).
9. Margaret Smith, *al-Ghazali, the Mystic* (London, 1944), pp. 13–14 (based on Tāj al-Dīn al-Subki's *Tabaqāt al-Shāfi'iya al-Kubrā* [Cairo, 1968], 6:193).
10. Quoted in Rahman, *Islam*, p. 130.
11. I. Goldziher, *Introduction to Islamic Theology and Law* (Princeton: Princeton University Press, 1981), p. 134.

Chapter 2/The Religious Valuation of Medicine

1. Muhammad Iqbal, *Kullīyāt* (Collection of Persian Poems) (Lahore, n.d.), p. 284.
2. *Mishkāt*, p. 436 (Robson, p. 1065).
3. Al-Tirmidhi and Ibn Māja, *Ṣaḥiḥ*, chapter on "Civil Wars."
4. *Mishkāt*, p. 421 (Robson, p. 1031).
5. *Mishkāt*, pp. 425, 424 (Robson, pp. 1039, 1038).
6. For similar Ḥadīth, see *Mishkāt*, p. 423 (Robson, p. 1035).
7. *Mishkāt*, pp. 421, 422 (Robson, p. 1031).
8. For this and similar Ḥadīth, see *Mishkāt*, pp. 422, 424, 425 (Robson, pp. 1033, 1036, 1039).
9. Muslim ibn al-Ḥajjāj, *Ṣaḥiḥ*, chapter on "Greetings of Peace." Another Ḥadīth says that a woman who had a cat which she starved to death was sent to hell (al-Bukhāri, *Ṣaḥiḥ*, chapter on the "Beginning of Creation."
10. *Mishkāt*, pp. 423, 425 (Robson, pp. 1035–36, 1039).
11. Ibn 'Arabī, "The *Fāṣṣ* of Hūd," *Fuṣūṣ al-Ḥikam*, ed. 'Afīfī (Cairo, 1946); English trans., *The Bezels of Wisdom*, by R. W. J. Austin (New York: Paulist Press, 1981), p. 137.
12. Quoted in Rahman, *Islam*, p. 155.
13. Ibn Khaldūn, *al-Muqaddima* (Cairo, 1867), p. 412.
14. See *Islamic Medicine* (Kuwait: Ministry of Culture, 1981), pp. 358–62.
15. See *Mishkāt*, p. 385 (Robson, p. 945).
16. Al-Dhahabī, *al-Ṭibb al-Nabawī* (Cairo, 1961), p. 6.
17. Maḥmūd Diyāb, *Kitāb al-Ṭibb wa'l Aṭibbā'* (The Book of Medicine and Doctors) (Cairo, 1970), p. 103; Ibn Qayyim al-Jauzīya, *al-Ṭibb al-Nabawī* (Cairo, 1978), p. 260.
18. *Mishkāt*, pp. 388, 389 (Robson, pp. 947, 949–50); see also Introduction to Ibn Qayyim al-Jauzīya, *al-Ṭibb*, p. 29.
19. Fazlur Rahman, *Prophecy in Islam* (1958; reprint, Chicago: University of Chicago Press, 1979), p. 45.
20. Al-Dhahabī, *al-Ṭibb*, p. 115.
21. *Mishkāt*, p. 137 (Robson, p. 327).
22. Ibnā Bisṭām, *Ṭibb al-A'imma* (Medicine of the Imams) (Najaf, 1965), pp. 16, 6.
23. Fazlur Rahman, "Islam and Health," *Hamdard Islamicus* 5 (Winter 1982):86.
24. For this distinction, see, for example, *Encyclopaedia of Islam*, s.v. *djihād* (*jihād*).
25. Published in Cairo (n.d.), pp. 3–4. The work was also known as *al-Kitāb al-Malakī* (The Royal Book).
26. Al-Sha'rānī's work was published on the margin of al-Majūsī's work (mentioned in n. 25 above), p. 3.
27. 'Abd al-Raḥmān al-Azraq, *Tashīl al-Manāfi'* (Cairo, 1963), p. 3.
28. Al-Bukhārī, *Guide for Students* (Meshed, Iran: Meshed University Press, 1965), p. 14 (italics mine).
29. Adolf Fonahn, *Zur Quellenkunde der Persischen Medizin* (Leipzig, 1910); Manfred Ullmann, *Die Medizim im Islam* (Leiden: E. J. Brill, 1970); Felix Klein-Franke, *Vorlesungen über die Medizin im Islam* (Wiesbaden, 1982).

Chapter 3/The Prophetic Medicine

1. Rahman, *Prophecy in Islam*, p. 56.
2. Diyāb, *Kitāb al-Ṭibb*, p. 103. A good deal of myth has undoubtedly built up around al-Ḥārith, and some contemporary historians of Islamic medicine have therefore dismissed the story of his having studied at Gundaishāpūr as spurious. Independent confirmation of al-Ḥārith's account is offered, however, in the earliest biography of the Prophet, which tells us that al-Ḥārith's son al-Naḍr was wont to sit in the place of the Prophet Muhammad, when the Prophet left after public preaching—wherein he often narrated biblical stories—and told ancient Iranian legends, saying, "How is Muhammad superior to me, for whereas he tells biblical stories, I recount Iranian stories." Certainly, then, al-Ḥārith and his son had an intimate connection and familiarity with Iran. Al-Tabarī, *Tārīkh al-Rusul Wa'l-Mulūk* (History of Prophets and Kings) (Cairo, 1969), 1:193.
3. Ullman, *Die Medizin*, p. 185.
4. Al-Dhahabī, *al-Ṭibb*, p. 3.
5. For Ibn Qayyim, see *al-Ṭibb*, pp. 73, 453; for al-Surramarrī, see Ullmann, *Die Medizin*, p. 187.
6. Ibn Qayyim, *al-Ṭibb*, pp. 73–74.
7. Al-Dhahabī, *al-Ṭibb*, pp. 139–40.
8. Al-Dhahabī, *al-Ṭibb*, p. 140.
9. Al-Azraq, *Tashīl*, pp. 3–4.
10. Al-Dhahabī, *al-Ṭibb*, p. 3.
11. Al-Dhahabī, *al-Ṭibb*, pp. 107–108; Al-Shāfi'ī is also credited with knowledge of medicine by al-Dhahabī and by al-Azraq (*Tashīl*, p. 3).
12. Al-Azraq, *Tashīl*, p. 3.
13. Al-Dhahabī, *al-Ṭibb*, pp. 143–44.
14. Al-Dhahabī, *al-Ṭibb*, p. 6.
15. Al-Dhahabī, *al-Ṭibb*, p. 7.
16. Al-Dhahabī, *al-Ṭibb*, p. 103; Ibn Qayyim, *al-Ṭibb*, p. 75.
17. Al-Dhahabī, *al-Ṭibb*, p 35; Ibn Qayyim, *al-Ṭibb*, p. 170.
18. *Mishkāt*, p. 134 (Robson, p. 325).
19. Introduction to Ibn Qayyim's *al-Ṭibb*, pp. 27–28.
20. Al-Dhahabī, *al-Ṭibb*, pp. 103, 104.
21. Klein-Franke, *Vorlesungen*, pp. 120ff.
22. Al-Dhahabī, *al-Ṭibb*, p. 103.
23. Ibn Qayyim, *al-Ṭibb*, p. 76.
24. Fazlur Rahman, "Islam and Medicine: A General Overview" *Perspectives in Biology and Medicine* 27 (Summer 1984): 593.
25. Ibn Taimīya, *Majmū' Fatāwā* (Collected Works), 2d ed., "Rabat," by the late King Khalid of Saudi Arabia, 24:275 (cf. Klein-Franke, *Vorlesungen*, p. 35).
26. Ibn Taimīya, *Majmū'* 24:275; 18:13.
27. Ibn Qayyim, *al-Ṭibb*, pp. 70–73.
28. Ibn Khaldūn, *Muqaddima*, pp. 346ff.
29. Ullmann, *Die Medizin*, p. 295.
30. References in n. 26 above; Ibn Qayyim, *al-Ṭibb*, pp. 222ff.

31. Ibn Qayyim, *al-Ṭibb*, pp. 171–72; all works on Prophetic Medicine cite this report.
32. For example, al-Qifṭī, *Akhbār al-Ḥukamā'* (History of Medical Men) (Cairo, 1908), p. 113.
33. See Ullmann, *Die Medizin*, chap. on Prophetic Medicine.
34. Al-Dhahabī, *al-Ṭibb*, pp. 112–13.
35. *Mishkāt*, p. 342 (Robson, p. 837).
36. Al-Dhahabī, *al-Ṭibb*, pp. 112, 113.
37. Trimmingham, *Sufi Orders*, pp. 125–26.
38. Quoted in Rahman, *Islam*.
39. Al-Dhahabī, *al-Ṭibb*, pp. 158, 159.
40. Fazlur Rahman, *The Philosophy of Mullā Ṣadrā* (Albany: SUNY Press, 1975), p. 223.
41. Al-Dhahabī, *al-Ṭibb*, p. 159.
42. Al-Dhahabī, *al-Ṭibb*, p.160.
43. Muḥammad Iqbāl, *Bāl-i Jibrīl* (Gabriel's Wing) (Lahore and Karachi, 1962), p. 181.
44. Al-Dhahabī, *al-Ṭibb*, p. 161.

Chapter 4/Medical Care

1. *Mishkāt*, p. 133 (Robson, pp. 320–21).
2. Al-Dhahabī, *al-Ṭibb*, pp. 145, 144.
3. *Mishkāt*, pp. 138, 139 (Robson, pp. 331, 333).
4. Al-Dhahabī, *al-Ṭibb*, p. 146.
5. *Mishkāt*, p. 136 (Robson, pp. 326–27).
6. Al-Dhahabī, *al-Ṭibb*, p. 146.
7. W. Heffening, *Encyclopaedia of Islam*, 1st ed., s.v. "*Waḳf;*" George Makdisi, *The Rise of Colleges: Institutions of Learning in Islam and the West* (Edinburgh, 1981), pp. 237–38.
8. Heffening, "*Waḳf.*"
9. Heffening, "*Waḳf.*"
10. Ziaul Haq, *Landlord and Peasant in Early Islam* (Islamabad: Islamic Research Institute, 1977), pp. 118, 125.
11. Heffening, "*Waḳf.*"
12. Heffening, "*Waḳf.*"
13. Otto Spies, *An Arab Account of India in the Fourteenth Century, being a Translation of the Chapters on India from Al-Qalqashandī's Ṣubḥ al-A'shā* (Stuttgart, 1936), p. 29.
14. An exception is the great shrine of its founder, Mu'īn al-Dīn Chishtī (d. 1236), at Ajmer. The Chishtī's tomb, still an object of pilgrimage for hundreds of thousands of Muslims (and Hindus), was endowed with vast lands as *waqf* in the sixteenth century by the Mogul emperor Akbar after his wife gave him a son at this central Chishtī lodge whither Akbar had sent her during her pregnancy for the shaikh's blessing. He named his son, also his successor, after the then-shaikh Salīm of the lodge.

15. Muhammad Mujeeb, *The Indian Muslims* (London: Allen and Unwin, 1967), pp. 74–75, 141–42
16. Amin A. Khairallah, *Outline of Arabic Contributions to Medicine* (Beirut, 1946), pp. 62–63. The translation from the original is my own as Khairallah's translation is rather clumsy (see the original in the Arabic version of the same work [Beirut, 1946], p. 73).
17. Bedi N. Šehsuvaroğlu, *Encyclopaedia of Islam*, new ed., s.v. "*bīmāristān.*"
18. Khairallah, *Outline* (Arabic version), p. 70 (quotation from Ibn Abī Uṣaibi'a, *'Uyūn al-Anbā' fī Tabaqāt al-Aṭibbā'*, has been omitted from the English version of the *Outline*).
19. *'Uyūn al-Anbā'*, quoted in Khairallah, *Outline* (Arabic version), p. 70; also Aḥmad 'Īsā, *Tārīkh al-Bīmāristānāt f'l-Islām* (History of Hospitals in Islam) (Damascus, 1939), pp. 15ff.
20. Ibn Abī Uṣaibi'a, *'Uyūn al-Anbā'*, pp. 198, 203–4.
21. Khairallah, *Outline* (English version), p. 61.
22. Khairallah, *Outline* (English version), p. 61.
23. 925 is the date of al-Rāzī's death. For the discrepancy involved—982 being the date of the opening of the 'Aḍudī hospital—see *Encyclopaedia of Islam*, new ed., s.v. *bīmāristān*. There seems to be some confusion in the name of the hospital, possibly between the 'Aḍudī hospital of 'Aḍūd al-Daula and that established by the caliph al-Mu'taḍid in the early tenth century.
24. Khairallah, *Outline* (English version), pp. 64–65; for a somewhat different version of the story, see Aḥmad 'Īsā, *Tārīkh*, p. 210, where it is said that a Persian gentleman of learning and taste, after seeing the magnificent hospital and its richness, wanted to test the people in charge of the hospital, feigned illness, and entered the hospital.
25. Ibn Abī Uṣaibi'a, *'Uyūn al-Anbā'*, pp. 731-32.
26. Aḥmad 'Īsā, *Tārīkh*, pp. 151–52.
27. Evliyā Çelebī, *Seyāhatnāme* 1:321–22, 468–70; 9:542.
28. Ševki, *Turkish Medical History* (Istanbul, 1925), p. 120; for the whole discussion see pp. 118ff.
29. Ibn Abī Uṣaibi'a, *'Uyūn al-Anbā'*, p. 604.
30. Khairallah, *Outline* (Arabic version), p. 81.
31. Muhammad Zubayr Ṣiddiqī, Introduction to *Studies in Arabic and Persian Medical Literature* (Calcutta, 1959), pp. xxxii–xxxiii, xxix.
32. Ṣiddiqī, Introduction to *Studies*, p. xxxvi; 'Alī Kauthar Chāndpūrī, *Aṭibbā'-i 'Ahd-i-Mughlīya* (Doctors of the Mughal Period) (Karachi, 1960), p. 87.
33. Ṣiddiqī, Introduction to *Studies*, p. xxxvi (illus. at p. xxxiii).
34. Cyril Elgood, *A Medical History of Persia* (reprint, Amsterdam, 1979), pp. 353–54.
35. Elgood, *Medical History*, pp. 354–55.
36. Ullmann, *Die Medizin*, p. 311.
37. 'Ali Aḥmad Nayyir Wāsiṭī, *Ṭibb al-'Arab*, 2d ed. (Lahore, 1969), p. 514.
38. Chāndpūrī, *Aṭibbā'*, p. 61.
39. Wāsiṭī, *Ṭibb*, pp. 519, 516.
40. Chāndpūrī, *Aṭibbā'*, pp. 143, 141, 142.
41. Chāndpūrī, *Aṭibbā'*, pp. 101–2.
42. Chāndpūrī, *Aṭibbā'*, pp. 103–6.

43. Chāndpūrī, *Aṭibbā'*, p. 41 (cf. p. 119).
44. I understand that a translation by Barbara Metcalf has been completed, but it is not yet published.
45. E. G. Browne, *Arabian Medicine* (Cambridge: Cambridge University Press, 1962), p. 40.
46. Huseyin Atay, *Osmanlilarda Yüksek Dīn Eğitimi* (Higher Religious Education among Ottomans) (Ankara, 1983), pp. 32ff., 87, 97.
47. Fazlur Rahman, *Islam and Modernity* (Chicago: University of Chicago Press, 1982), p. 35.
48. Wāsiṭī, *Ṭibb*, p. 517.
49. Browne, *Arabian Medicine*, p. 41.
50. Ullmann, *Die Medizin*, pp. 225–26; Wāsiṭī, *Ṭibb*, pp. 257ff. Wāsiṭī contends that the examination of doctors had begun much earlier than al-Muqtadir's time with the official funding of medical schools and that what al-Muqtadir did was to establish a system of medical registration.
51. Ibn Abī Uṣaibi'a, *'Uyūn al-Anbā'*, p. 731.
52. Wāsiṭī, *Ṭibb*, p. 259.
53. The following account is in Wāsiṭī, *Ṭibb*, pp. 259ff.
54. Wāsiṭī, *Ṭibb*, pp. 263ff.
55. Ibn Hishām, *Sīra* 1:358.
56. Michael W. Dols, "Insanity in Byzantine and Islamic Medicine," in *Symposium on Byzantine Medicine*, ed. John Scarborough, Dumbarton Oaks Papers, no. 38 (Washington, D.C., 1984).
57. *Chahār Maqāla* (Tehran, 1970), p. 126; for the second story, Ibn Abī Uṣaibi'a, *'Uyūn al-Anbā'*, p. 188.
58. Al-Rāzī, *The Spiritual Physick of Rhazes* (London, 1950).
59. Al-Rāzī, *al-Sīra al-Falsafīya* (Tehran, 1964), pp. 91–103. This treatise was published by Paul Kraus with a French translation and introduction under the title *Raziana 1 in Orientalia*, vol. 4 (1935).
60. Al-Rāzī, *al-Sīra*, p. 92.
61. Al-Rāzī, *al-Sīra*, pp. 93, 102, 103.
62. Rahman, *Major Themes of the Qur'an*, chap. 3.
63. Niẓām al-Dīn, *Fawā'id al-Fu'ād*, Urdu trans. Muhammad Sarwar (Lahore: Auqaf Department, Government of the Punjab, 1973), p. 250.
64. Chāndpūrī, *Aṭibbā'*, p. 129.
65. This copy exists in the private collection of Muhammad Ḥusain Jalālī, Chicago.
66. Katherine Ewing, *Pirs and Sufis in Pakistan* (Ph.D. diss., University of Chicago, 1980), pp. 74–75.

Chapter 5/Medical Ethics

1. *Kitāb al-Mustaṣfā* (Cairo, 1904), 2:350.
2. Rahman, "Islam and Health," pp. 80–81.
3. This whole controversy arose from the Qur'anic verses in which the Prophet (along with other prophets) is made to say that he only teaches and preaches for God's sake and asks for no money in return (in 26, 109, 127, 164, 180; 34, 47, etc.) and also from the verses in which Jewish rabbis are accused of "selling God's verses for a paltry sum of money" (2, 174; 3, 77, 187, etc.).

4. I know from personal experience as a young man that this was a hotly debated question among the 'Ulamā, including my father. Those who were not in favor of accepting a fixed salary allowed acceptance of voluntary gifts. It is well known that many Sufis in particular preferred destitution to prosperity and that, for example, Shaikh Niẓām al-Dīn, when he accepted gifts, also gave gifts in return but never accepted gifts of land in support of his hospice. He accepted only gifts like food and money that could be distributed immediately among the poor. See Mujeeb, *Indian Muslims*, pp. 134–35, 141–42.
5. Al-Dhahabī, *al-Ṭibb*, p. 110.
6. Ullmann, *Die Medizin*, p. 225.
7. Al-Ruhāvī's work was translated into English by Martin Levy as *Medical Ethics of Medieval Islam* (Philadelphia, 1967).
8. Rahman, "Islam and Health," p. 81.
9. Rahman, "Islam and Health," pp. 81–82.
10. Ullmann, *Die Medizin*, p. 224.
11. Introduction to *al-Ṭibb*, by Al-Rāzī, ed. 'Abd al-Laṭīf al-'Īd (Cairo, 1978), pp. 24–25.
12. Al-Rāzī, *al-Ṭibb*, p. 25.
13. Browne, *Arabian Medicine*, p. 52.
14. Ullmann, *Die Medizin*, p. 224.
15. Niẓāmī-Ye 'Arūẕī, *Chahār Maqāla*, pp. 106, 113–14.
16. Niẓāmī-Ye 'Arūẕī, *Chahār Maqāla*, pp. 108–9.
17. Al-Rāzī, *al-Ṭibb*, p. 33.
18. Al-Rāzī, *al-Ṭibb*, p. 37.
19. For example, Niẓāmī-Ye 'Arūẕī, *Chahār Maqāla*, pp. 121–23.
20. Al-Rāzī, *al-Ṭibb*, pp. 53ff.
21. Al-Rāzī, *al-Ṭibb*, pp. 58ff., 41.
22. Al-Rāzī, *al-Ṭibb*, p. 122.
23. Al-Rāzī, *al-Ṭibb*, p. 123.
24. Al-Kirmānī's critique of al-Rāzī's *Golden Sayings* (*al-Aqwāl al-Dhahabīya*) was published along with al-Rāzī's text (pp. 169ff.).
25. Al-Rāzī, *al-Ṭibb*, p. 59.
26. See Fazlur Rahman, "Human Rights in Islam," in *Democracy and Human Rights in the Islamic Republic of Iran* (Chicago: Committee on Democracy and Human Rights, 1982). Mimeo.
27. For the following account, see Fazlur Rahman, "Status of Women in Islam," in *Separate Worlds: A Study of Purdah in South Asia*, ed. L. H. Papanek and G. Minault (Columbia, Mo.: South Asia Books, 1982).
28. For Muslim family law see Fazlur Rahman, "A Survey of Modernization of Muslim Family Law," *International Journal of Middle East Studies* 12 (1980): 451–65.
29. *Encyclopaedia of Islam*, s.v. *mut'a*. For the current situation in Iran, see Shahlā Hā'erī, "The Institution of Mut'a Marriage in Iran," in *Women and Revolution in Iran*, ed. Guity Nashat (Boulder, Colo.: Westview Press, 1984).
30. For the following discussion, see references in nn. 27 and 28 above.
31. This doctrine is based on certain Ḥadīths which say that expensive shrouds should not be provided to the dead because living people need cloth more than the dead. According to the Shāfi'ī school of law, if a pregnant woman is dying, her

baby should be extracted from her womb if it has a good chance of survival. See, for example, Ibn Qudāma, *Kitāb al-Mughnī* (Cairo, 1968), 2:410, 411, 525.
32. Ibn Qayyim, *al-Ṭibb*, p. 312.
33. Al-Shaibānī, *al-Jāmiʿ al-Ṣaghīr*, section on *al-iqrār bi'l-nasab* (acknowledgement of parenthood.)

Chapter 6/Passages

1. For this discussion, see Bāsim F. Musallam, *Sex and Society in Islam* (Cambridge: Cambridge University Press, 1983), pp. 39ff., 46, 50.
2. Musallam, *Sex*, pp. 46, 39.
3. Musallam, *Sex*, p. 50.
4. *Mishkāt*, p. 293 (Robson, pp. 719–20).
5. Rahman, "Islam and Medicine," pp. 591–92.
6. The *Khuṭba* of ʿAmr ibn al-ʿĀṣ, in *Tārīkh ʿAmr ibn al-ʿĀṣ* (Biography of ʿAmr ibn al-ʿĀṣ), by Ḥasan Ibrāhīm Ḥasan, 2d ed. (Cairo, 1926), pp. 140–41; Abul Ḥasan Zaid Fārūqī, *Islam and Family Planning*, 3d ed. (New Delhi, 1976), p. 68.
7. Rahman, "Islam and Medicine," p. 592.
8. Musallam, *Sex*: for Islamic law, pp. 57–59; for medical practice, pp. 69–71.
9. Rahman, "Status of Women," p. 290.
10. Rahman, "Islam and Medicine," p. 592.
11. Musallam, *Sex*, pp. 57–59.
12. A good view of this multifaceted picture of sexuality can be obtained from *Society and the Sexes in Medieval Islam*, ed. A. L. al-Sayyid-Marsot (Malibu, Calif.: Undena, 1979).
13. This more crass side of sex has recently been portrayed (with vengeance) by Fatna A. Sabah in her *Woman in the Muslim Unconscious* (New York: Penguin, 1984).
14. Annemarie Schimmel, "Eros—Heavenly and Not So Heavenly—in Sufi Literature and Life," in *Society and the Sexes in Medieval Islam*, ed. A. L. al-Sayyid-Marsot (Malibu, Calif.: Undena, 1979), p. 130.
15. Ibn ʿArabī, *al-Futūḥāt al-Makkīya*, 9 vols. (Cairo, 1911), 4:84.
16. This is one of the grounds on which a woman can seek divorce, called *khul*ʿ. See the various compendia on Islamic law s.v. *khul*ʿ; see also references in nn. 27 and 28 in chap. 5.
17. *Mishkāt*, p. 268, (Robson, p. 606).
18. *Mishkāt*, pp. 309ff. (Robson, pp. 781ff.).
19. Fazlur Rahman, *Islamic Methodology in History* (Karachi, 1965), pp. 182ff.
20. *Mishkāt*, p. 286 (Robson, p. 704).
21. *Mishkāt*, p. 287 (Robson, pp. 704–5).
22. Mahmood Ibrahim, "Social and Economic Conditions in Pre-Islamic Mecca," *International Journal of Middle East Studies* 14 (1982): 351–52.
23. Fazlur Rahman, "The Concept of *Ḥadd* in Islamic Law," *Islamic Studies* 4 (1965): 242.
24. *Mishkāt*, pp. 250ff. (Robson, p. 709).

INDEXES

NAMES

SUBJECTS